Educational Controversies

What is the purpose of education? This question lies at the heart of the debate between academics, educators, politicians, and parents, resulting in a never-ending series of opinions and solutions. Often, it seems that opposing interests, the desire for a "quick fix," and changing political climates result in a stalemate situation, where issues remain unresolved.

The authors of this unusual and provocative book believe, however, that the solution to overcoming differences lies in finding a new approach to the process of debate. Drawing on personal and professional experience, they demonstrate their theory by looking at several key areas of controversy in education, including:

- How should children learn?
- What should children learn?
- How should learning be assessed?
- How should parents choose their children's schools?

Within these areas the authors describe a path of reconciliation by finding common themes and inter-relations and by providing strategies for developing productive, democratic debate. Researchers, educators, students, and education policy makers will all find this a challenging and stimulating book and a powerful antidote to the argument culture.

Pamela LePage has worked for four years as an Assistant Professor of Education at George Mason University and is now the Director of the Committee on Teacher Education at Stanford University, California, USA. **Hugh Sockett** is a Professor of Education in the Department of Public and International Affairs at George Mason University, Virginia, USA.

Educational Controversies
Toward a discourse of reconciliation

Pamela LePage and Hugh Sockett

London and New York

First published 2002
by RoutledgeFalmer
11 New Fetter Lane, London EC4P 4EE

Simultaneously published in the USA and Canada
by RoutledgeFalmer
29 West 35th Street, New York, NY 10001

RoutledgeFalmer is an imprint of the Taylor & Francis Group

Typeset in Goudy by Taylor & Francis Books Ltd
Printed and bound in Great Britain by The Cromwell Press,
Trowbridge, Wiltshire

British Library Cataloguing in Publication Data
A catalogue record for this book is available from the British Library

Library of Congress Cataloging in Publication Data
Sockett, Hugh.
Educational controversies : toward a discourse of reconciliation /
Hugh Sockett and Pamela LePage.
p. cm.
Includes bibliographical references and index.
1. Education–Aims and objectives. 2. Learning–Educational change.
I. LePage, Pamela
LB14.7 .S64 2002
370.11 21   2001045730

ISBN 0–415–27066–9

Contents

Acknowledgements

We owe particular thanks to all those who have commented on this book and the ideas within it, especially those who attended our presentations at the American Educational Research Association, the American Association of Higher Education, the American Association of Colleges of Teacher Education, and the Intellectual Life of Schools Summer Conference 2000 at George Mason University.

We are particularly grateful to Teresa Byard, Kelly Decker, Jim Finkelstein, John Robinson, Ann Sevcik, Robert Smith, Alan Tom, and Diane Wood for their consideration and care in reading the manuscript in one or other of its iterations. We are grateful to our readers at RoutledgeFalmer who provided such helpful comments.

We also wish to thank the *Washington Post* for permission to reprint two articles: "Divided on Connected Math: For Some Parents and Experts, Curriculum Doesn't Add Up" (October 17, 1999) by correspondent Brigid Schulte, and "Oklahoma's Divisive Disclaimer on Evolution" (December 1, 1999) by correspondent Lois Romano.

Finally, we owe especial thanks and love to our respective spouses, Ann Sockett and David Lees, who have both borne the trials of living with a writer with their usual good humor and support.

Fairfax 2001

Introduction
The challenge to improve public education

Introduction

It would be difficult to find co-authors of a book on education with educational backgrounds as diverse as ours. Pamela moved all over the United States as a child in the 1970s and attended more than 15 different public schools by the time she graduated from high school. Hugh went to a private boarding school in England during the 1940s and 1950s where he was taught (among other things) how to speak proper English. Pamela remembers young teachers in bobs and beads. Hugh remembers young teachers back from the war in Burma or Berlin. Pam remembers as a child watching the horrors of Vietnam on television. Hugh recalls nights in shelters or under the dining room table while bombs and later rockets fell on England's industrial heartland. Pam attended San Diego State University as an undergraduate. Hugh attended the University of Oxford. Pam never took a philosophy class during her entire school career. Hugh believes that philosophy is at the heart of every discipline.

Our present views of education were not just delivered to us by our school teachers. While young Hugh was being hit over the head (sometimes literally) with content (large books), Pam's elementary school teachers were striving to make her feel good about herself; she remembers singing, playing games, and drawing pretty pictures. Our colleges also had different orientations. Pam's education had a vocational emphasis. Students at San Diego State were taught how to be teachers, how to be social workers, and how to be engineers. At Oxford, arguably the most famous university in the world, the "dons" (as professors were known) were mostly interested in students enjoying intellectual struggle. Crudely, their view was if you didn't master content from your discipline, and become well read and knowledgeable, you wouldn't produce any insightful argument.

Our educational backgrounds represent very different emphases on the aims of education. They invite questions such as: What is appropriate to teach children? What is important to know? Should we emphasize one aim over another? If Hugh doesn't remember being taught to feel good about himself, why is he now so confident? If Pamela never remembers intellectual struggle, how did she learn to do this?

Whatever our differences, we are now both dedicated to improving educational opportunity, and seeking to contribute to that through the writing of this book. Both of us have published traditional academic texts, but we search here for a style which combines our passions for the topic with the usual rigors of disciplined writing. The process has been especially valuable for us. Our diversity brought us together intellectually. Our differences fed our thinking on this topic. The collaboration in this book is an example of how people who are very different can learn from each other and build upon strengths. Additionally, in the summer of 1997 two baby boys were born six weeks apart. Garrett is Pam's son. Jack is Hugh's grandson. Those events brought us together emotionally. These two boys have a reasonable expectation of surviving to 2080. Their children will probably witness the dawn of the twenty-second century. We talked about the wonder, privilege, and excitement of being parent and grandparent and wondered how these two boys might gain from our experience and study. Will they be exposed to the emphases in education that we thought important in our history? Will they have the opportunity to experience what we thought was missing? What were our educational hopes and aspirations for them?

As this conversation developed, our experience as professional educators told us that nothing much would have changed in education before Jack and Garrett finish college because none of the profound debates about education will have been resolved. Educational transformation seems out of reach, whatever the claims of new movements and new emphases. What struck us most forcibly is that the stalemate and lack of progress arises primarily because public education is a battleground. No one seems interested in working out solutions, merely in fighting old battles. We need a new kind of conversation. We therefore decided to write this book primarily as an invitation to all those who:

- share our frustrations at the lack of progress and dismay at the ideological battleground the schools have become;
- look for solutions to problems which are shared, not routinely heap blame on opponents; and
- will experiment in their schools, colleges, associations, or churches, even their families, with the new ideas for the process of discussion we will outline.

This book is idealistic. In it we search for a new style of democratic conversation about education with a promise of educational improvement. We have rejected the scramble for the lowest common denominator and work to avoid yet another swing of the infamous educational pendulum. We have abandoned the traditional kind of argumentative debate, seeking to build up a discourse of reconciliation between the different and contradictory aims and purposes people have for education. We want people to listen to each other, to figure out how our political and educational institutions can draw on *all* that is valuable from the corpus of human thought about education. We define the overall task as follows:

- to examine controversial aspects of the different aims of education;
- to suggest ways in which they may be reconciled by looking for inter-relations, mutual dependencies, and links of importance between positions;
- to articulate educational aims and purposes in a way that might help all educators understand better what they do at both a practical and an ideological level;
- to develop procedures to enable any reader with an educational interest – a teacher, a parent, a grandparent, a caregiver – or someone concerned about discussion in our society, to contribute more effectively to public debate and to making private individual judgments; and
- to provide suggestions for developing nurturing and supportive learning communities.

We begin in this introductory chapter by describing five obstacles to educational improvement, which have occasioned our concerns and which, we believe, lay the foundation for unproductive discourse. In this introductory chapter, our style and tone is forthright, meant to evoke an emotional response, which contrasts with our search for reconciliatory discourse that follows through the book. Whether our own arguments are passionate or antagonistic, reasonable or unreasonable, will depend on the reader's perspective. For, if a reader agrees with a writer, the work is often described as passionate. If s/he disagrees, it is viewed as antagonistic. So it is a constant struggle to create a balance between antagonism and passion and between legitimate criticism and propaganda.

Chapter 1 then articulates the *core* of what we have come to call reconciliatory discourse and why we think it is needed. We specifically emphasize the twin pillars of moral trust and intellectual struggle as its foundation, believing that both are crucial in resolving problems, which invariably reveal conflicts in basic educational aims.

In Chapter 2, we will use the example of fierce argument about the mathematics curriculum. We print a newspaper report on this topic, which reveals all the primary aspects of antagonistic discourse we would like to see changed. From that we construct an agenda for the development of a reconciliatory discourse, while grounding the argument securely.

In Chapter 3, we then describe the step-by-step *procedure* that provides a discussion framework, concentrating on the intellectual form of the discourse, which we also spell out as a protocol in the Appendix.

In Chapter 4, we take another example of educational controversy, namely competition and collaboration, and we search the content of the debate for ways in which protagonists could construct a common problem for solution.

However, both the issue of mathematics and that of competition and collaboration raise the question of whether all positions can be reconciled and what will be necessary, by way of attitude, habit, and commitment of participants in reconciliatory discourse. This forms the content of Chapter 5.

Each of Chapters 6–8 then deals with one area of intense controversy in an attempt to delineate how antagonisms might be better understood and what might be possible by way of reconciliation:

* How should the schools that children attend be chosen (school choice)?
* How should children's learning be measured (standardized tests and authentic assessment)?
* What should children learn (the content of the curriculum)?

In Chapter 9, we seek to connect our educational insights, driven by the arguments we will have suggested for educational reconciliation, to matters of value and motivation with respect to educational purposes. We conclude with a brief summary of the political, social, moral, and civic need for a new stance to debate and what we see as the way forward. The Appendix is very important. It describes a protocol, built on the procedures, for use in a formal discussion context. Our stance is not to provide a recipe, but to develop a model which others can use.

Five obstacles to improving education

It is an immensely complicated task to build a public education system worthy of a sophisticated industrial democracy. We should not be surprised that many problems beset public education in the United States at the beginning of the millennium. However, we discern five to be of particular importance since they each affect debate and educational practice for the worse. These are:

* the conflict of educational purposes;
* the poor quality of public debate;
* the lack of public access to the language of education and intellectual struggle;
* the power of special interests; and
* the lust for the quick fix and the consequent dynamic of the swinging pendulum.

Yet underpinning every educational discussion is the fact that everyone has been to school. Everyone can therefore correctly claim knowledge and experience, if not expertise. There is a strong tendency in all of us to want our children taught the same way because we are familiar with the way we have been taught. This applies to everything about schooling from learning multiplication tables to choosing a college, and even to the use of the paddle ("corporal punishment never did me any harm"). Any innovation in education can seem suspect and contentious. People used to believe that schooldays were "the happiest days of your life," which meant simply a freedom from adult responsibilities. That was always a suspect cliché, for school is not just any experience, it is an *emotional* experience. "Most adults," writes Nancy Franklin, "would check the box next to 'You couldn't pay me enough to go through that again'" (*New Yorker*, October 18 and 25, 1999, p. 232).

Indeed, being forced to attend school, being "taken away" from our family as a youngster, has a huge impact on us as individuals. At day care for some, at school for all, we encounter a public environment for the first time. All kinds of undesirable experiences can occur – humiliation, rejection, a sense of one's own incompetence, the angst of growing up, physical shame, and being ridiculed among them. There are desirable experiences too, as Pat Hersch (1998) has so vividly described. For teenagers in some urban areas, the high school is an oasis. The cafeteria, the hallways, and the bathrooms are the only safe places in the neighborhood for adolescents to congregate. Many come to value the comradeship and opportunities for friendship that are provided just by being in a school. Some relationships prove to be long lasting. Wistfully perhaps at high school reunions, we recall our different selves and our changed friends, a theme portrayed in such varied frameworks as Philip Roth's *American Pastoral*, and the movie *Peggy Sue Got Married*.

The impact our schooling has had on us, for better or worse, means that few people are emotionally neutral about schooling. Debates about education get an immediate emotional charge because of our own experiences. When we become parents or caregivers, that charge is intensified. No one should be surprised, for example, by parents arriving in the principal's office enraged by what *they perceive, indeed see* as harm being done to their children by teachers. Antagonism is fueled by emotion, especially for those who do not see themselves as valued by the school. Moreover, if Deborah Tannen is right, much of our education consists in being taught how to be antagonistic (Tannen, 1998, Chapter 9). Confrontations seem constant and almost unavoidable. They are reflected in the five problems we see as harmful to public education.

Conflicts of educational purpose

Our primary concern is that the character of the debate surrounding educational purposes often obliterates any attempt to reconcile them. For the past 200 years, three perspectives on educational purposes have emerged, which can be boiled down to one of three basic assumptions:

- education prepares people for their social role;
- education develops people as individuals; or
- education gives people knowledge of their culture.

We refer to these divisions of purpose throughout the book as society, self, and knowledge. It is rare to find people advocating that public education fulfill only one of these functions. Usually, there will be a major emphasis on one, with an acknowledgement that the others have a subsidiary place in the education of the nation's children. (For a complex critical account of this division of purposes, see Egan, 1997.)

This simple three-fold distinction can get complicated, since within each category there are differences and disagreements. For example, where the emphasis is on preparing people for a social role, some argue for a *specific* vocational purpose (e.g., training for automotive work), others for a *general* socializing purpose (e.g., working in learning communities where social experience and getting along with other people become paramount). Where the emphasis is on the individual, some believe that education should make children feel good about themselves, while others argue that the individual's relationship to God is pre-eminent. Finally, where the emphasis is on knowledge and culture, conservative thinkers argue for a canon, or the basics, or core knowledge for every child, whereas some progressives believe that children construct knowledge and can do that only through the articulation of their own experience.

None of these three main educational purposes is likely to disappear – they are always in tension. That, we believe, is inevitable in a democratic society. There will always be different views of what education – particularly public education – should be in a democracy. Its content, organization, structure, and purposes are all legitimate and important areas for debate. Yet the conflict between them, in many different forms, is pursued as a conflict which, as we suggest in Chapter 9, is out of date in the contemporary world.

From these differing educational purposes and the practice of schools there emerge "oppositions." Here are some examples:

- In elementary education there is a major rhetorical and political battle between those who believe that phonics teaching is essential in teaching children to read and those who see literacy as a matter of whole language acquisition. The State of California in 1998 legislated phonics to be the method for teaching reading.
- The "back to basics" movement (whether that be a matter of core knowledge in curriculum or advocacy of an instructional mode of teaching) is pitted against those who would argue for relevance and experience as children construct knowledge.
- Influenced by behavioral psychology, cognitive psychology, brain research, multiple intelligences theory, and vocational education are the advocates of thinking skills and mental processes, who are opposed by those with philosophically grounded views of knowledge and knowing.
- There seems, too, to be an irreconcilable difference between those who see the school as a caring community and those who see it as a place to socialize children into the American way of life.

Self-esteem, left and right brained, cooperative learning, multiple intelligence, multi-culturalism: the list of ideologies, positions, and posturing seems endless. Of course, some will object to the way we have articulated these ideologies as oppositions, claiming that many are positions embedded in overlapping categories. We agree. The point is that many educators view them as oppositions and relate to them in this way, which affects practice.

The poverty of public debate

The quality of public debate about education and educational purpose is an important obstacle to its improvement. Cheap talk, as Professors Guttman and Thompson (1996) put it, drives out quality talk.

From the university, to the national debate, to regional, state, and local forums, discussion is almost entirely antagonistic (Tannen, 1998). People approach the debate from prepared positions out of old conceptions rooted in a general emotional commitment, or out of the kinds of special interests we have identified. The pattern is to "conceptualize issues in a way that predisposes public discussion to be polarized, framed as two opposing sides that give each other no ground" (p. 11). Moreover, journalists, politicians, and others who lead public discussion, sustain educational controversy. Forensic, antagonistic argument is portrayed as "real" public democratic debate (see Tannen, 1998, Chapter 2).

Take a typical TV discussion. The chairperson, whatever her/his background, has to be an entertainer. That is, s/he is looking for *entertaining* lively combative discussion to hold the audience. The more successful the combat, the better the entertainment, the more remuneration for the entertainer, and the continuing flow of advertising revenue. "It's head to head competition, not over anything as rarefied as depth of analysis but simply over attention grabbers," wrote Walter Goodman in a devastating critique of TV punditry (*New York Times*, December 9, 1998). Program designers and TV executives choose people for the program who are articulate, quick on their feet, and full of the art of aggressive body language. All the chosen contributors will have a financial stake in a TV debate, the purpose of which is not to resolve a conflict but to sustain it. A journalist with a syndicated column across a hundred or so newspapers needs to sustain her/his "position" for that is why newspapers across the country buy what s/he has written. Careful argument is discounted. This may seem overly cynical. In 1988, however, Hugh appeared with Al Shanker (formerly President of the American Federation of Teachers) in a lunchtime talk show. The entire context seemed to have been set up so that the issues were largely ignored. As it was Hugh's first time doing this sort of thing in the United States, he felt he was terribly inept. Going down in the elevator afterwards, he said as much to Shanker who was sympathetic but comforting with the phrase "Don't worry, Hugh, it's only entertainment."

This combative model so constantly displayed is then deployed at all levels across the nation. Politicians, journalists, or pundits on the lower rungs need to move up the ladder by becoming adept at the skills of antagonism. There are some notable exceptions to this style, but the financial motive seems to reach wide and deep. The Editor of *US News and World Report*, James Fallows (1997), argued that "talking heads" were now celebrities rather than reporters finding their own stories. Moreover, some were earning $30,000 a speech and earning up to $6 million a year. They were more interested in sustaining conflict and controversy, he suggested, which gets in the way of discussion and compromise. At all levels of discussion about the future, in all types of public life, the dominant mode of conversation is one of conflict, fed, it would seem, by financial self-interest.

Just as self-interest comes into public discussion on TV, so it also comes into academic educational debate. Individuals in universities frequently spend time articulating, and then defending, a position, sometimes over the years and in the face of decisive criticism. They struggle to create a voice that will be listened to among a cacophony of differing opinions. Institutional pressure supports this discourse, for professors are judged *inter alia* on how well they can argue or defend their position. They are rarely judged by how well they can reconcile their position with another. This can then become materialist in motive. If I have an educational idea, I become a huckster, as William James described it. I have a product I have to sell, especially as it is on one side of a given conflict. I will keep on plugging away at the competition in the market place. I am not going to seek some form of reconciliation with my "competitors." Just as conflict is our political bread and butter, so it is in academic life. Special interests frequently look to academics for theoretical justifications, whether that is for specialist education, the gifted and talented, prayer in schools, or whatever. As academics ourselves, by the way, we are conscious that in writing this book, our self-interest is involved. We hope we are not coming across as "holier than thou" because we freely admit that the two of us constantly struggle with opening ourselves up to those with whom we disagree. Hugh has been criticized for being categorical. Pamela has been criticized for being blunt. We find no problem ourselves in admitting to either description, but both represent different challenges in our personal quest to seek a reconciliatory style and intellectual habit.

The lack of public access to educational language and intellectual struggle

We also think there is a strong case for arguing that academics have stolen intellectual conversation and shut many ordinary citizens out of the debate. This is a strong claim, so look at a comparable example. Levine (1990) uses the final scenes of the Marx brothers' film *A Night at the Opera* to suggest that working-class Americans were enraged by the way in which opera, as part of their culture, had been hi-jacked as a high-brow pursuit. As you may recall, the brothers create mayhem on the stage. But, you will ask, was opera really a low-brow pursuit – ever? Now recall the production of Mozart's *The Magic Flute*, as shown in the film *Amadeus*, for a clear notion of opera being a delight and a possession of the common person, a genuine part of popular culture.

Our case is different. Educational discourse in the twentieth century has been stolen by academics because they have made it impenetrable to the ordinary person. They have filled it with terminology, drawn from behavorist psychology, Rogerian therapy, neo-Aristotelian theory, and postmodernism, which clouds public discussion. "This society," wrote Ford Foundation's Peter Stanley, "suffers terribly from the separation that is opening between it and its most thoughtful members" (Boyer, 1990, pp. 69–70). Some contemporary educational movements, home schooling for example, express a similar kind of rage and anger to that shown by the Marx brothers in their parody of the opera. At the political level, Chester Finn's (1991) book is titled *We Must Take Charge!* And a common reaction to academics is disdain. As one of the country's leading former superintendents said to Hugh recently, "You know, I think that the vast majority of what you education academics do is bullshit!" Somehow authentic educational discussion has to be accessible to every citizen, let alone every superintendent. That can't happen if people feel blinded by science.

We might go even further. The impenetrability of jargon-laden language has taken away from people the possibility of intellectual struggle. In American society, often a few intellectuals (e.g., academics) take wisdom and claim it as their own. They hold it close to them as if they own it, but could lose it anytime. Then they organize it, analyze it, digest it, and spit it back out as a recipe for the masses to follow. Or worse still, they proclaim a notion of subjectivity in which anything anybody does is as good as the next person's, thereby draining the notion of struggle or effort from the enterprise. Sadly, educational bureaucracies continue the thievery by providing tests that emasculate intellectual struggle by making it a demand on the memory, not the intelligence, creativity, or imagination.

The power of special interests

Inside and outside education, the "children in the middle" seem to be neglected. This is not because teachers want to ignore them, but because schools are constantly bombarded by special interests. Countless "types" of children are identified for special treatment: the gifted and talented, children with special needs, ADHD (Attention-Deficient Hyperactivity Disorder), and so on. Historically, there is an important reason for this. In the past, the needs of children on the margins were not being adequately considered. Therefore, pressure groups arose to influence policy makers. These policy makers, with teachers, spend energy and time trying to determine which group is most needy, what focus will produce the greatest number of well-educated people, and how to distribute resources to satisfy the special interests. Maybe the lobbies that constitute these special interests in a democracy are an inevitable consequence of social complexity, but pragmatic, complex, and fair solutions are often drowned out by the clattering of hobbyhorse hooves.

The child-focused special interest group is only one type within education. Another type is the professional special interest represented by such organizations as the American Federation of Teachers, the American Association of School Administrators, and many others. A third, more influential, type comprises those so-called experts and journalists financially committed to the continuing promotion of argument and debate. They have an interest in continuing an educational debate that pits groups against each other, for resources, for attention, or for special treatment.

The quick fix and the pendulum effect

The massive self-confidence of Americans carries with it the old Greek sin of *hubris* (overweening pride), the belief that American is exceptional (Lipset, 1996). For example, the American consumer is highly privileged in world terms. We expect satisfaction now! People approach schools with a similar mind-set. Fix my child! Children sometimes have the same attitude. Go on, teach me! Antagonism is fueled because both ordinary people and public protagonists alike seem to believe a monstrous illusion – the illusion of the educational quick fix! It is fed by such educational/political sound-bites as "All Children Can Learn" and "Johnny Can't Read."

We get easily attracted by quick fixes and education has seen them come and go – teaching machines, radio, educational TV, and now the Internet as a curriculum elixir for schools. School-board members in search of re-election, as well as other politicians, bureaucrats, and journalists alike, often pressure superintendents, administrators, and teachers (anxious to appease constituents) into addressing highly complex problems with simplistic solutions. But contrast that with Connecticut, where Jay Mathews (2000) writes:

> Connecticut and its local school boards provide some of the highest teacher salaries in the country, mentors for every new teacher, exhaustive checks of classroom competence, extra help for the lowest-performing schools, early intervention with poor readers and a patience and consistency rare since the state of education became a favorite issue for American politicians. "The striking thing about Connecticut is its commitment to a series of reforms over a long period of time," said Lynn Olson, project editor for the annual "Quality Counts" reports on state education changes published by the newspaper *Education Week*.
>
> (*Washington Post*, July 18, 2000, A.11)

Systems are driven by political forces, which sometimes run against the personal convictions and educational ideals of individual administrators. Where they are in concert, the logic of operation is the long hard slog, not the quick fix, as Connecticut is demonstrating.

But there is an old joke among teachers that if you stay in the same place, you'll probably be an educational innovator twice in your career! Steady improvement in education seems to be impossible because of the pendulum effect primarily generated, we believe, by the press of antagonistic interests. The pendulum effect is a story about change in education. Testing provides a good example:

> As the last decade of the century unfolds, there is more educational testing occurring than we have ever witnessed before. Like many other educational phenomena, however, testing seems to fall in and out of favor in cyclic fashion over time. Usually the era of peak demand is followed by a period of increasing criticism of the inadequacies of testing and of the inability of tests to address our most pressing educational problems. By decade's end, we likely will have come full circle from the 1970's when charges of racial/ethnic bias dominated our thoughts and contributed to a decrease in educational testing.
>
> (Ebel and Frisbie, 1991, p. 1)

This 1991 prediction seems to have come true. Pick up any newspaper at random these days and a person is likely to find headlines about teacher testing, or content-based tests for Standards of Learning (e.g., *Washington Post*, January 14, 1999). The present rush is for standards and testing. As in testing, so in other parts of education where a political, academic, or professional group is always ready to show that it can do something – *now*. An existing practice is castigated, and a new or an old idea, depending on the context, is elaborated in opposition. Searching for the elixir of improvement, school boards and superintendents force schools to swing from one position to the other, sometimes without a clear understanding of the rationale, and, in the case of state mandates, often privately convinced the latest elixir is badly mistaken. Nevertheless, teachers are then given a quick course in the new fad or fashion, and off they go to teach it.

Conclusion

The emotional baggage of everyone's own schooling, the political character of educational special interests, the poverty of public debate, the lust for the quick fix and the swinging pendulum, and the citizen's lack of access to educational jargon each reflect an *apparent* three-fold, deep-rooted conflict of educational purpose. Frankly we don't believe the conflicts need be so hysterical, nor do we believe all oppositions are incompatible. Rather, it is the manner in which debate is conducted that is so damaging. Deborah Tannen's (1998) wide-ranging diagnosis of the argument culture is perhaps the best known. Amy Guttman (Princeton) and Denys Thompson (Harvard) have been searching for ways to provide a procedure for solving intractable public controversies in a democracy (Guttman and Thompson, 1996). From Europe, philosopher Jürgen Habermas (1994) has been calling for a "public sphere," a space where the private person can get a word in edgeways. James Sears and James Carper (Sears, 1998) have brought together people from diametrically opposed social positions (e.g., on abortion and religion in schools) to seek for common ground.

Donald Schon and Martin Rein (1994) have developed a complex process based on the principles of design to find frames of analysis for public policy issues. We are not therefore alone in our concern about public discussion.

Yet, some people will reject this rough analysis of the problematic character of antagonism out of hand. They will not want to enter the democratic debate searching for agreements, but for power. Others see democratic polities as an arena for figuring out ways of imposing one's will on others. Others are so opinionated that they believe a discussion is a place where one should state a position and then turn one's back. Forensic debate is deeply rooted in our education (see Tannen, 1998, Chapter 9). Many politicians, as we have hinted, make a living out of dissent. We think that Americans are being insulted and demeaned by the different ways in which a search for reconciliation is ignored in the pursuit of winning, especially when it is argued that *it is not in the self-interest of many people in America to search for a reasonable common ground.* As Thomas Boswell puts it: "In a culture that, every year, seems to define itself more in terms of raw competition, we are tempted unconsciously to reduce issues to 'I'm a winner. You're a loser'" (*Washington Post*, November 28, 1999).

For us these are not just academic matters upon which we professionally pontificate. As parent and grandparent we are mightily upset. We don't want Jack's and Garrett's education to become a political football. We long for a climate of positive discussion, in which different and contradictory views can be respected, examined, and thought about intelligently. We want to think with other people about the strengths of a point of view, rather than its weaknesses. We believe a discourse of reconciliation, not antagonism, can be created which will be morally much more productive. It is a major undertaking to change our orientation in public debate away from winning and antagonism to finding common ground through reconciliation. However, we don't accept the argument, usually made by those trapped in the quick fix mentality, that this is a utopian ideal or that it will never happen across the nation. Of course it's a long haul, and will yield very small gains very slowly. We must gradually abandon the antagonistic idea that the sole purpose of debate is to win at all costs.

Yet this chapter has hardly been written in a reconciliatory tone: so we as authors need to set an example by putting our passions into a different frame. The frame is the process of searching for common ground, which we call the discourse of reconciliation, the central vision of which is the focus of the next chapter.

1 A new vision of educational debate

Reconciliatory discourse

We strongly believe that teaching is a fundamentally moral occupation and that the approach to resolving educational controversies should be set in a moral frame (Sockett, 1993). In this chapter, we first outline the vision of reconciliatory discourse, anticipating its detailed description in Chapter 2, and we show its connection to the three educational purposes that were described in the introductory chapter. In the second section, we locate its foundations in the twin notions of moral trust and intellectual struggle. From these underpinnings will come a view of reconciliatory discourse, which demands the meeting of hearts as well as minds. The aim is to rethink the purpose of educational debate, within the commitment to build on the best to improve education for all children. To do this, there will be the development of common ground on aims, the use of compromise, an ability to build on the best of arguments, and to integrate them.

Reconciliatory discourse and educational aims

Etzioni (1996) has suggested rules of engagement to make dialogue more constructive. They include not demonizing those with whom you disagree, not affronting their deepest sensibilities, talking less of rights and more of needs, leaving some issues out, and engaging in a dialogue of convictions (pp. 104–106). These seem to us valuable, and we build on these ideas, as well as Tannen's (1998), as we strive to delve deeper into the character of discourse in terms of solving common problems. We seek to go beyond Tannen's analysis and Etzioni's precepts, advocating what we call reconciliatory discourse. We define it in the following way:

> Reconciliatory discourse (RD) is a civil discussion in which participants with divergent views seek to build common ground for (educational) practice through the articulation of a shared problem to which they are all morally and intellectually committed. Participants in RD use compromise and make practical choices to build on the best. They respect divergence and eschew consensus for consensus' sake. They use its principles in writing as well as in practice-oriented discourse. Their purpose is to make better public and private judgments about education.

RD does not therefore provide solutions to controversial questions. It is a procedure for helping people with different points of view mutually define a problem, while sophisticating their judgment in the process. The emphasis on defining the problem arises from our conviction that in educational debate agreed solutions are impossible because protagonists do not share a common problem (see Chapter 2), and "it is important to name the problem precisely because all the work to follow will be directed at correcting the problem as it has been named" (Kepner and Tregoe, 1997, p. 29). Exchanging solutions to differently conceived problems is not likely to improve public education. Yet the search for the common problem has also to be driven by "doing the conversation right." If we "do it right," the problem we define (and the eventual solution) will be "right." This won't be because we found the true answer or some brilliant insight about how to solve a problem. Rather, we will have struggled morally and intellectually, under the best conditions, working toward the best solution possible.

However, we did not set out to describe merely a procedure for conversation. We are practically motivated by the question, how can we reconcile the aims of education? For example, how can we find ways for teachers to both teach content and encourage self-awareness? How can we teach children to question authority, while also socializing children into American culture? Reconciling aims is not a matter of taking down strategies from a shelf. It emerges from conversation. The way to bring the diverse aims of education together is deeply embedded in reconciliatory discourse. We are working to reconcile aims by seeking to understand what is best in different points of view, especially when the heart of the disagreement is embedded in people's beliefs about the purpose of education.

There will be many ways people might design a reconciliatory conversation. We have outlined a procedure and tested it on a number of "oppositions" (see Chapter 3), which will no doubt be refined and changed as we work with it. Yet such discourse needs an underpinning, which we believe is a *moral* basis of trust and an *intellectual* basis of struggle. Both will demand a different mind-set about other people, trusting that they care and have moral motives. It will demand seeing those with whom we disagree not as being wrong, but as people with important ideas that need to be carefully considered. There will be a premium on collaboration.

Trust and struggle: the core of RD

At its core, RD has both a moral and an intellectual base. Most people would have no difficulty with the intellectual, but may find the moral much more confusing. The confusions arise from four main sources. First, many believe that being a moral person must derive from religious beliefs. Second, many believe that to express a moral viewpoint is merely to express an opinion, and an opinion is by definition merely subjective. Third, many believe that morals are relative, differing from society to society or from age to age, so that any form of moral condemnation of another society cannot be warranted. Finally, many equate the moral with very limited categories of human experience, for example sexual behavior.

This is not the place to counter all these confusions in detail but simply to say that, as with many serious misconceptions, there is a kernel of truth lurking in each of them. First, those with religious beliefs do draw implications for their (moral) acts and actions from their religious beliefs and, as in most versions of Christianity, regard their behavior as following God's instructions. But this cannot be the case for those who live exemplary moral lives (e.g., Socrates), but have no serious religious beliefs. People don't have to be religious to be moral. Second, while it is essential that a moral person act from her/his own will (rather than under orders), that does not mean that the moral beliefs the person has or the opinions s/he expresses are merely opinion. The general belief, for instance, that "you ought to keep your promises" is widely accepted as a moral principle. It's not just my opinion that you ought to keep your promises.

Third, while it is true that there are dissimilarities between many societies on certain things, the treatment of women for example, there are many areas in which there is moral congruence (e.g., the need to care for the sick). If we focus on our individual moral views, we risk ignoring the moral character of a community and the similarities between such communities (Etzioni, 1996). Finally, to think of moral behavior as referring to just private and inter-personal sexual matters is to ignore the moral issues of honesty, fairness, courage, justice, trust, loyalty, and so on. "Too many people," quipped an English raconteur, Malcolm Muggeridge, "have sex on the brain," which, he added, "is a terrible place to have it."

Educational thought is influenced by these confusions as, for example, where teachers feel they dare not "impose their values" on children. The central problem, however, is that educational thought is not primarily conceived as moral, but technical thought, even though the central purposes of the educational endeavor are moral. The language of education is also weakened because the moral concepts that are needed have been neglected. If a person thinks education is mainly a technical business (like fixing a space ship), s/he will talk the talk of the technicians and engineers. Their language arises from scientific facts about the world, not from human understanding of humanity. But if a person believes, as we do, that education is a moral business, her/his language will be different. In technical language, children are often discussed as a type (gifted and talented) or a statistic (black under-achiever) or indeed as just a role (e.g., a third-grader). With a technical orientation, a person might explain "how to" fix, or control, or teach these types (e.g., give them stickers when they are good). A moral orientation means that a teacher's work should be viewed as a profession, which presents difficult moral choices that need constant consideration, experimentation, and reflection (Sockett, 1993). It means understanding teaching and learning not through the dominant psycho-technical concepts, but through terms like fairness, courage, determination, effort, honesty, and value (see Chapter 9).

Indeed if educational discussion were rooted in moral, not technical language, it could be more accessible to the ordinary person. Writers on educational topics in the academic world have many assumptions and schemata within which they couch their prescriptions for practice such that the research world sometimes seems more like the Tower of Babel than the ivory tower! Academics understand the language of psychologists, critical theorists, and cultural feminists; but the ordinary person may not understand "metacognition" or "standardized tests." Yet they have some understanding of trust, laziness, courage, concentration, commitment, and so on. If more people felt they had access to educational language, talking about it would not therefore become less complicated or sophisticated. But it could mean that more people would talk to each other coherently within a common language, which RD might provide.

Why reconciliation, exactly? Many people would think of reconciliation as the kind of upshot from a couple visiting a marriage guidance counselor. We specifically use the word reconciliation and the term RD because we want to emphasize the personal within educational debate. As a parent and a grandparent, we are not merely participants in a theoretical argument, but people actively searching for a framework that will influence decisions that deeply affect those we love. Sure, we seek to build "common ground," but we want reconciliation on that common ground. Compromise too, with its sense of a "middle way," isn't enough to describe what we want either. Common ground and compromise, of course, find a place within our notion of reconciliation. But you can compromise out of fear, not in a spirit of reconciliation (see Tannen, 1998, p. 99). You can find common ground as a practical matter, but not take it seriously. Reconciliation, to repeat, demands a meeting of hearts as well as minds. It suggests commitment. It reconciles people as well as the ideas and the aims they have for education. For us, reconciliation captures the moral character and style of the discourse we envisage. It is about people and their children, *not* about *ideas about* people and their children. No one can enter RD just as an exercise (academic or otherwise).

In RD, the main moral concept is trust and the main intellectual concept is struggle.

Trust and the moral base

Reconciliation makes demands. It involves a preparedness to see one's wants and desires as not overriding. It particularly demands trusting other people. Trust carries with it some degree of selflessness. What is trust? Trust, Hugh says, describes a relationship between two or more people (Sockett, 1993). Characteristic of a relationship of trust will be four features:

- A person can predict accurately how the other will behave, primarily because s/he shares some wants, goals, aspirations, or ends with this other person.
- A person must believe the other person has goodwill and is rational.

- Those who trust each other must be in constant conversation and dialogue.
- Both must be dedicated to reflection and self-examination within the trusting relationship.

So those who trust each other can examine their own acts and thoughts from the perspective of trust. The moral aspect of RD in practice demands the creation of trust, whereas antagonism often feeds mutual distrust. Trust is interpersonal and authentic. You can't have exercises in trusting someone else, just as you can't plan to be sincere, although interestingly, you can practice antagonistic strategies of debate. But the goal is not to resolve conflicts, because conflict can be the impetus for change and conflicts can be resolved without any particular need for further trust. RD can use conflict to propel us forward by giving us a way to work through opposed positions productively.

Struggle and the intellectual base

RD will demand intellectual struggle as well. We suggested that such struggle has been taken away from people (see page 8). Embedded in any effort, any struggle, is the possibility of failure. Struggle thus carries with it recognizing (intellectually) that you could be wrong.

We have both been surprised by how readily many teacher–students we have worked with initially accept the erroneous idea that knowledge is somehow uncomplicated. Indeed, they seem to resist the idea that working with knowledge is messy, confused, lacking in clarity, and contradictory. In other words, they resist the idea that working with knowledge is a *struggle*. When we were discussing how teachers can reconcile the aims of education, we considered the idea that teachers often focus on presenting factual content *or* they focus on reflection *or* they work to socialize children. What seemed to be missing was the glue that held these different educational purposes (self, society, and knowledge) together, a way to integrate them appropriately. We believe the glue is what we call "intellectual struggle."

Writing this book and working out our ideas has itself been an intellectual struggle. For example, in doing our first draft of the chapter on testing and authentic assessment (see Chapter 7), a number of questions came up about the reconciliatory process as we wrote to apply it to testing. So we asked ourselves, should we go back and iron out the inconsistencies in our procedures and try hard to present a perfectly articulated model for RD? We did try to iron out some problems. Yet we then decided that it would also be helpful to describe our thinking process as we worked through the procedure, because we wanted to give the reader a chance to follow along with us in our struggle and hope that it will provide something of a model.

The particular struggle was the effort to reconcile educational aims as we grappled with the idea of the procedure for a new kind of talk. We were trying to convince people to approach educational controversy differently (the social purpose), we were trying to integrate our personal experiences (the individual purpose), and we struggled with educational content presented by a number of scholars in the field (the knowledge and culture purpose). We realized we were not just plotting a discourse, but working to reconcile the diverse aims of education. We have concluded that the drive for reconciliation demands intellectual struggle, not just the arts and crafts of holding back, resolving a conflict, or negotiating a treaty. When people (especially students) struggle intellectually, they go through a process of reconciling intellectually or morally diverse points of view. For teachers, these "points of view" will be grounded directly in the three different educational aims and purposes or practices that embody them.

Explore this idea from a different perspective. If a teacher simply presents information that students must memorize, students are not getting inside the material and seeing its depth. If s/he has students write a reflective piece and they simply describe their own experiences, more often than not, it has little depth because it is not informed by the experience of other people, alive, dead, or fictional. If s/he asks students to write a theoretical essay about a serious social issue and all they do is spout "their opinions," the essay will be shallow. If, however, students take some serious content in depth, connect it profoundly to their lives and experiences, and explain in depth how it can influence society, they will have succeeded in the intellectual struggle the topic presents, and they will, in different ways, be fulfilling the three different educational purposes.

The distinctive character of RD

We referred earlier in the chapter to the choice of the word reconciliation as being distinct from compromise or the common ground but we suggested both had some place within this discourse. How is reconciliation different from compromise? How is reconciliation different from taking a centrist view? How is reconciliation different from doing a little of everything in an effort to please all parties?

These questions have been asked of us a number of times since the beginning of the project. After we finished working through each of the reconciliation examples (see Chapters 2, and 5–9) we found that reconciliation is the frame for any and all of these possibilities. We found from some of these chapters we had drafted that ultimately we would:

- Use the expertise on both sides to either create a new strategy or build upon the old. Work together to develop something new (as in Chapter 2).
- Do both and build on the best of both arguments and address the concerns of both sides (as in Chapter 6).
- Make a compromise that builds on the best of both arguments and addresses the concerns of both (as in Chapter 4).
- Make a choice based on the best argument and incorporate the best attributes of an opposing position (as in Chapter 7).
- Adopt an integrated approach where the aims are meant to build on each other (as in Chapters 8 and 9).

Our central argument for the distinctiveness of RD, therefore, is that while we may choose to compromise, to integrate different views, or to choose a middle way, these choices are not made on pragmatic or expedient grounds. Reconciliation has its roots firmly planted in the idea that no matter what option we choose, we should be building on the morally and intellectually best in the different positions, such that we can each embrace the choices made.

Additionally, although we are working with oppositions, and we have developed a procedure, it is not our aim to provide people with a way to choose accurately between two existing solutions. We are not trying to list the pros and cons so that we can decide which one is best. We believe we can best elaborate the procedure we recommend by opening up completely new possibilities by carefully examining features of existing conflicts. Barrett (1997) describes something similar when he defines paradoxical thinking, which he believes helps people think about solutions in new and interesting ways. The goal in RD is to explore ideas that have not yet been considered, not simply debate familiar positions. The point is not to find some test or metric that helps us choose between the two (or five, or whatever) choices we have, but to examine these supposedly fixed, opposed positions and develop something different and hopefully better. We are not simply proposing another procedure for problem analysis. We advocate changing the common approach to controversy in education, from antagonistic to moral. Specifically, we are attempting to provide strategies for:

- engaging in productive, moral conversations;
- defining a problem more accurately; and
- opening up new possibilities for alternative solutions.

Reconciliation and research

New patterns of discourse will move educational progress forward and stop the pendulum. We can, and certainly should, seek out statistics and qualitative research, anecdotal examples, and polls to try to understand the nature of the problems we face. And we need to set high standards for evaluating empirical evidence, as we have endeavored to do in the past. But we are not working to find some test or metric to help us choose between the alternative positions because there are no ultimately reliable tests or metrics that can remove all human judgment (Polanyi, 1962). So we need to accept the frailty of social science evidence and embrace (rather than resist) the reality that educational decisions are mostly based on human judgment.

The process is extremely ambiguous. In the twentieth century, social scientists had hoped that subjecting social problems to "rigorous scientific research" would give us correct answers to our questions. We need to reconceptualize the task of research where we see it as reconciliatory in potential. For public debate is served by educational research, where its purpose is to find answers to questions in the public domain. For RD, we need evidence to support claims, but we also need to acknowledge the limitations of research in the humanities and the social sciences (see Stearns, 1993, Chapters 2 and 3). A reconciliatory approach would define the research goal as one of understanding what is best in different positions, a classic example of which is to be found in the reconciliation of Skinner, Freud, and Piaget as contributors to understanding a child's moral development (see Peters, 1974, Parts I and II). Research becomes a type of reflection and synthesis, alongside and perhaps leading the customary empirical models of testing of hypotheses in a controlled experimental process. Such reconciliation in research might feed public discussion more productively.

Conclusion

Public education in a democracy is not merely a moral business, but is inherently political. In our political culture, sometimes, what is done is reconciliatory. We experiment with solutions in various contexts and we use what we learn from (often failed) experiments to better understand the nature of our problems. We should respect minority rights even in a majority decision. Our decisions necessarily involve competing groups. If we understand this complexity and embrace it going in, instead of arguing vigorously for one "pure" solution or another, we will make much better decisions and have a lot less pointless conflict.

In this book, as we have said, we want to provide a model, not a recipe. The model will be of two kinds. We have already stated that we will set out the procedures (Chapter 3) and model its use with a number of controversies. We have also explained that this book itself presents a model of reconciliation of the three educational purposes (self, society, and knowledge). As authors, we have learned (and presented) a great deal of "content" (knowledge). We have worked to convince people to use a reconciliatory approach (society), and we have incorporated our personal experience (self). In addition, reconciliation is modeled through our collaboration. Although we have different styles and backgrounds, we endeavored to build on the best of our strengths as collaborators. In sum, we present a set of procedures for RD outlined in Chapter 3, but we also present a model of reconciliation in the book itself, both in terms of demonstrating the reconciliation of educational purposes and the reconciliation of styles in collaboration.

We have described the underpinnings to our vision of RD. In Chapter 2, we examine an example of antagonism and from it begin to build a procedure for RD in Chapter 3.

2 The problem and the vision
The battle over math education

The real challenge in producing change lies both in articulating problems and posing theoretical solutions, and in providing the means by which the change can be implemented. To begin the process of understanding the complexity of RD and working toward this idealistic vision, we have reprinted a *Washington Post* article below that details a controversy surrounding contemporary debate on math education for children. We then make some preliminary observations before using this example as a way to start thinking through a reconciliatory procedure, to determine the types of information people will need to reconcile a conflict, and to struggle with the complexity of what it means to move away from antagonism toward reconciliation.

"Divided on Connected Math"

Under the headline "Divided on Connected Math: For Some Parents and Experts, Curriculum Doesn't Add Up" (*Washington Post*, October 17, 1999) correspondent Brigid Schulte reported:

For anyone who hated math in school, didn't get geometry or grumbled, "What's the point of a quadratic equation?" James Koutsos's sixth-grade math class is a revelation. On a recent day, after organizing pairs of students to play a tick-tack-toe-like game about prime numbers and leading a spirited class activity on Venn diagrams using popular radio stations, he asked his students what they thought.

A forest of hands shot up. "Oooooh. Oooooh. Pick me!"

"The game helped me learn to multiply and divide," said a boy named Jason.

"It was hard to win," said a boy named Darin, draped in baggy jeans and a skull T-shirt. "It's just fun to do."

Fun? Math?

Koutsos and his class at Montgomery County's Col. E. Brooke Lee Middle School are part of an experiment. Lee is one of five county schools testing a new way of teaching math. What is going on in Koutsos's classroom is at the heart of a passionate, often vitriolic debate that has shot through school districts nationwide and has now reached Montgomery.

The program is called Connected Math. It aims to have students actually understand math and how it is used. To understand, for example, that a quadratic equation helps demographers project population trends and Red Cross relief workers estimate how many tents they'll need for a refugee camp.

To do that, Connected Math breaks loose of the drill-and-kill way math has been taught for ages. It attempts to engage all students, not just the 15 percent who always have done well, by relating math to the world they live in. Thus, percentages are taught with story problems about restaurant tips and the sales tax on CDs. Fractions, ratios and perimeters are taught within the context of movie tickets, brownies and bad cat breath.

Students play games, write in math journals and often work together in small groups. They no longer sit in neat rows, all facing the blackboard, as the teacher lectures, scratching out the answers to one problem after another.

"An abomination!" said critic Wayne Bishop, a math professor at California State University. "Utter trash!" said Richard Askey, a prominent mathematician at the University of Wisconsin. It's MTV math. Placebo math. Mickey Mouse math.

Critics' biggest beef is that in the rush to imbue "deep conceptual understanding," Connected Math skips over the computing skills students need.

John Hoven, head of a group of parents of gifted and talented children leading the charge against Connected Math in Montgomery County, calls it "fuzzy math." "The students may be having a good time," he said. "But they're not learning anything."

On the surface, the war of words rages over the value of learning long division; the fact that while there is still one right answer, Connected Math allows for several ways to get there; and whether students learn best when the teacher lectures or students are left to discover answers on their own.

But the debate has near-religious undertones, which focus on fundamental and unresolved questions like: What is math? How do you teach it? And who gets to learn it?

To complicate matters, there is little solid, objective evidence – state scores, SAT scores – toward proving that either camp is right because the approach is so new.

"There are people who fervently believe math consists of computational skills and the way you do it is, someone shows you, then you practice, practice, practice," said Bill Jacob, a mathematician at the University of California at Santa Barbara. "Connected Math forces students to make sense of problems, to think. These are two very different views of the world. That's why there's such passion."

And heavy hitters choosing sides.

The U.S. Department of Education last week declared Connected Math one of five "exemplary" math programs. The American Association for the

Advancement of Science rated it number one. The president of the National Council of Teachers of Mathematics helped write it, and the National Science Foundation backs it financially.

But it also was rejected by California for failing to meet the state's rigorous new back-to-basics standards. Mathematically Correct, a parents group with a commanding presence on the Internet, gave it an F. And 600 parents in Texas are suing their school district for giving students no other choice.

Passions are running so high in Montgomery that the new superinten-dent, Jerry Weast, created an expert panel to mediate.

At a meeting of the group for parents of gifted and talented children one evening, Ray Russo, who has a doctorate in math, became agitated as he explained that Connected Math, to him, isn't math, it's math appreciation. "Math is symbolic abstraction and formal proof. It means you don't have to fool with objects," he said. "It makes my eyes light up."

But Nancy Metz, the county's math coordinator, who also taught math and was a mathematician in the aerospace industry, feels just as deeply. "If we are censored from trying this, and I fear that's what's going to happen," she said, tears brimming, "I will regret it as long as I live."

Ironically, both camps are motivated by a fundamental concern: that U.S. students perform abysmally on national and international math tests. In the latest international math comparison, high school seniors scored above their peers in only Cyprus and South Africa. And both sides agree that middle school math has, for years, been a wasteland. Students are able to compute or memorize formulas. But when faced with solving a story problem, they freeze. Many have no idea how to use what they know.

"We've had the longest-running experiment in human history about whether rote memorization of math facts and skills works. And it doesn't. Students are coming to universities and into the workplace not understanding math," said Glenda Lappan, president of the National Council of Teachers of Mathematics and one of the authors of Connected Math. "Why wouldn't I want to try something new?"

In Montgomery, 75 percent of seventh-graders passed the math part of the 1999 Maryland functional test, while 94 percent passed the reading test. Black and Hispanic students' reading scores lagged 10 percentage points behind their white and Asian counterparts; the gap yawned to 30 or more points in math.

"If anything, the math score should be equal to or better than the reading score in most places, because of language problems and the immigrants who have the tools to solve math prob-lems but don't have the language," Weast said. "I don't think there's any doubt we want progress in the math program. There's no doubt we need teacher training to do that."

A teacher training grant is what

sparked the controversy here. Patricia Flynn, director of academic programs for Montgomery schools, and other administrators applied for a $6 million grant from the National Science Foundation to help get more middle school teachers into college math classes and certified as math teachers. In Montgomery, 57 percent of the middle school math teachers lack secondary math certification, and 20 percent have not satisfied Board of Education college math requirements.

But Hoven and others protested that the grant would only train teachers the new way, which they say is aimed at low-performing students who don't get math at the expense of their children, who do.

Across the country, it is largely the parents of gifted children who are fighting Connected Math and similar programs. They fear two things: that forcing their bright children to work in groups with others will hold them back and that relating math to the world they live in won't boost their college-entrance SAT scores.

"The hidden secret of Connected Math is that some gifted students don't perform as well, and their parents become enraged," said Lynn Raith, mathematics curriculum specialist in the Pittsburgh school district, one of the first to test the program. "They were good at memorizing and moving numbers around, but if you asked them to explain something, they couldn't. Now, they have to think. But the truth is, once you win the children over, you win the parents over."

That didn't happen in the case of Cathy Berninger, a Montgomery parent of a gifted child who lived in a San Diego district using a similar approach. "We recognized very soon that our seventh-grade daughter was rapidly losing interest in her honors math class," Berninger said. "We basically had to hire a tutor for her."

With fears so basic and convictions so strong, Weast's expert panel is unlikely to end the war in Montgomery.

On Friday, the panel, which included a Nobel laureate, issued a short report, saying, in essence, that the county didn't treat the objecting parents very well but that the current math curriculum needs improvement and the critiques of Connected Math aren't convincing enough to keep it from classrooms.

Within hours, Hoven shot down the report.

Against this swirling backdrop, Steven L. Bedford, principal at Lee Middle School, has one simple goal, which sounds just like Hoven's: to use challenging programs like those used in Singapore and Japan to get more students into Algebra I by eighth grade. And to give them the foundation to do well on the SAT.

"Connected Math is just one more tool to get there. It's only a pilot. If it doesn't work, we'll try something else," Bedford said. "If what we're doing works for a small part of the population, let's keep doing that right. But if it's not working for everyone else, and it's not, let's not keep doing something that hasn't worked for 20 years."

In James Koutsos's sixth-grade class, over lunches of barbecued chicken, blue Gatorade and goldfish crackers, four 11-year-old students recalled once hating math.

"I just used to stare at my work. I was confused," said Candy Rosel. "The teacher would give an example, and I still didn't understand."

Now they write in their math journals about the "special numbers" they've picked, like 40, for a mother's age, and 18, for when they can leave home, and 24, because it's how many hours are in a day. They diligently list the factors and some multiples of each.

"This is good. It helps you learn in a fun way," said Chelsea Vogel. "Last year, we'd just sit in class and just talk about math. It was so boring." They listen to the teacher, Koutsos, then work in pairs. Then he summarizes what they've learned. The class likes that.

"It kind of feels good when you're helping someone out," said Shayla Hines, who for the first time is thinking about becoming a teacher, a math teacher, even. "It helps me know more, too."

New Math

Below are sample math problems that are being used as part of the Connected Math program for sixth-graders. The program is designed to make math more fun and accessible to students and is being piloted in Argyle, Col. E. Brooke Lee, Shady Grove, Silver Spring International and Sligo middle schools.

Problem 1

At Loud Music Warehouse, CDs are regularly priced at $9.95 and tapes are regularly priced at $6.95. Every day this month, the store is offering a 10 percent discount on all CDs and tapes.

Joshua and Jeremy go to Loud Music to buy a tape and a CD. They do not have much money, so they have pooled their funds. When they get to the store, they find that there is another discount plan available just for that day – if they buy three or more items, they can save 20 percent (instead of 10 percent) on each item.

A. If they buy a CD and a tape, how much money will they spend after the store adds a 6 percent sales tax on the discounted prices?

B. Jeremy says he thinks he can buy three tapes for less money than the cost of a tape and a CD. Is he correct? Explain your reasoning.

ANSWERS

A. They will spend $ 16.12. The solution involves several steps:
Step 1: Find the total cost before the discount: $9.95 + $6.95 = $16.90
Step 2: Compute the 10 percent discount: 0.1 x $16.90 = $1.69
Step 3: Calculate the discounted price: $16.90 - $1.69 = $15.21
Step 4: Compute the tax: 6% x $15.21 = $0.9126, which rounds to $0.91
Step 5: Compute the total cost including tax: $15.21 + $0.91 = $16.12

B. Jeremy is incorrect.
Step 1: Compute the cost of three tapes: 3 x $6.95 = $20.85

Step 2: Compute the 20% discount:
$20.85 x 0.2 = $4.17 and $20.85 x $4.17 = $16.68
Step 3: Compute the tax: 6% x $16.68 = $1.00
Step 4: Total cost is $17.68. This is more than the $16.12 for a CD and a tape.

Problem 2

Element portion of Earth's crust:
Oxygen 0.4660, Iron 0.0500, Silicon 0.2772, Aluminum 0.0813, Sodium 0.0283, Calcium 0.0363, Potassium 0.0259, Magnesium 0.0209.

A. Order the elements in the Earth's crust from most abundant to least abundant.

B. Estimate how much of the Earth's crust is made up of the three most abundant elements.

C. About what percent of the crust is made up of the three least abundant elements listed in the table?

ANSWERS

A. Oxygen, silicon, aluminum, iron, calcium, sodium, potassium, magnesium.
B. Oxygen + silicon + aluminum = 0.4660 + 0.2772 + 0.0813. This is roughly 0.85 (the exact answer is 0.8245), or about 85 percent.
C. Sodium + potassium + magnesium = 0.0283 + 0.0259 + 0.0209. This is roughly 0.08 (the exact answer is 0.0751), or about 8 percent.

Preliminary observations

This story demonstrates existing oppositions and the apparent difficulties people have in identifying a common problem and moving to a concerted solution. Shortly after it was published, an advertisement was printed in the *Washington Post* in which a large number of university professors of mathematics called for the US Department of Education to repeal its decision to make Connected Math one of the five "exemplary" math programs. This story provides an example of a controversy where both groups of people are dedicated to children's learning, yet because they have different philosophies about what and how children should learn, they have turned an intellectual puzzle into a personalized battle that causes pain and frustration for all involved. This seems a harsh reality for people who have dedicated their lives to improve mathematics education for children. The parties involved in this conflict, we believe, need RD. Let's begin by looking at the text in terms of our concerns expressed in the introductory chapter:

- Conflict of purpose. "Two very different ways of viewing the world," it is said, between those who "believe math consists of computational skills and practice," and those who "force students to make sense of problems." Two of the traditional divisions on educational purpose are represented (see page 5), between those who think of knowledge as the center of education and those who think of social purposes. Each would argue, in this case, that children were motivated and interested. Both are concerned by the place of American schools in international league tables, and wish to remedy it.

- The quality of public debate. Passionate, vitriolic, "a war of words rages," near-religious undertones, "heavy hitters choosing sides," tears brimming, "fears so basic and convictions so strong," a "swirling backdrop." From the academics, "an abomination," "utter trash," "placebo math," "fuzzy math." The rhetoric is very strong too: "the students may be having a good time, but they're not learning anything" is contradicted by the report's accounts of children's voices. The idea that the Mathematically Correct parents group gave it an F, and 600 parents in Texas are suing their school district for giving students no other choice, seems antagonistic.

- The lack of public access to educational language and intellectual struggle. At a meeting of parents of gifted and talented children, we are told, Ray Russo, who has a doctorate in math, became agitated as he explained that Connected Math, to him, isn't math, it's math appreciation. "Math is symbolic abstraction and formal proof. It means you don't have to fool with objects. It makes my eyes light up." How many, we wonder, would know what it is that makes his eyes light up?

- The power of special interests. The proponents who devised Connected Math aim to understand math as it is used, and to "engage all students, not just the 15 percent who have always done well," among which, of course, will be professors of mathematics. But it seems that the "group of parents of gifted and talented children leading the charge against Connected Math" indicates the power of special interests. Indeed "across the country it is largely the parents of gifted children who are fighting [note the word] Connected Math."

- The quick fix and the pendulum effect. A classic example of trying to quick-fix a deep-rooted problem is the "expert panel." It was called upon to mediate, but neither group seemed interested in mediation as such, because the debate focuses on "fundamental and unresolved questions like 'What is math?' 'How do you teach it?' 'And who gets to learn it?'" This particular example doesn't contain any obvious pendulum effect. In fact, some might argue that both groups are arguing from opposite ends of the pendulum. The problem is not to be solved by mediation between groups, as in conflict resolution, but by reconciling different educational aims through RD. There is obviously no sense of mutual trust, nor is there any real sense on either side of the importance of them struggling together with a problem. How can these two groups define a shared problem and work together to solve it?

Working toward a procedure of reconciliation

Right now we cannot reconcile the advocates' philosophies about math or math education, because that would involve many hours, if not days or weeks, of careful RD conversation with a number of people on both sides of the conflict. And it would be impertinent (and probably illegal) to put words into the mouths of the named advocates, adults or children, so we will be content with examining positions as they are presented in the article. So we are approaching this as if Jack and Garrett were going to school in Montgomery County. Be aware therefore that we are not approaching this quarrel as math educators, on which neither of us has expertise. We are trying to establish some central questions from examining this article to help us in the construction of RD.

Understanding the problem and locating the issues

As a place to start reconciliation, we first need to locate the issues. We need to understand the oppositions and their origins. Historically there has been a drill and practice view dominant in teaching mathematics to all children, "the longest running experiment in human history" as one proponent describes it. There is evidence to support the assertion that children are not learning math. The lack of understanding shown by undergraduates, the poor levels of adult numeracy, and the familiar international league tables show that the United States needs to address issues of learning and teaching in the area of math. Before educators began in the 1920s to figure out how to make math interesting to all children, it was simply accepted that bright children would lap it up and go on to algebra, calculus, statistics, and so on. The rest of us would gather the math we needed for everyday life. "Gifted and talented" children are, in part, defined as such by their mathematical ability as defined by computational skill. By definition, therefore, gifted and talented children are good at math. Nevertheless, as the country becomes heir to a knowledge-driven economy, it is more important from one viewpoint at least that more children not just "get it," but actually enjoy it – and the two are interconnected in learning. There has also been some "progressive" math education work that does not seem to have impacted children's performances for the better.

As we begin to understand the nature of the oppositions and can locate them, we need to also consider individual motivations. The ambitions parents of clever kids have for their children are not hidden in this article, though such individual motivations might often be concealed in other contexts. Yet parental ambition (which we of course share) is different from the nature of mathematics. This is not to discredit it, but to point out that it is a feature in RD, namely self-interest. Of course, if children are not taught "SAT" math, they're going to have a hard time doing well on the tests. There could be surrogate as well as hidden problems too (which do not exist on the data of this article): for example, someone could have started this ruckus to get a superintendent or principal fired.

Similarities and differences

Second, after we understand the history and location of the problem, and have probed the individual perspectives of the advocates, we need to enumerate the similarities and the differences of the positions. To do that, all concerned would need to temporarily suspend judgment and try to understand the positions from the alternative perspective, which looks to be very difficult as the advocates have declared their ground so strongly. There is nothing in the article which suggests that they might even be willing to search for understanding, try to see the other position from the inside, or look at the other person's position as objectively as possible. Yet it will be important in RD for the professional mathematicians to suspend judgment and ask, "Am I fully understanding what is being said – especially about the success this seems to be having in getting children interested in math?" Or for the Connected Math folks to ask, "Are we missing opportunities for abstraction and formal proof?"

The reality of all dialogue and argument is that it always involves power relations of some kind. The suspension of judgment can diminish them. In fact, trying to be heard, having a voice, and being part of the decision-making process are all different ways to talk about a "search for inclusion and power." The article reveals the central power relation, namely between the parents of the gifted and talented and some professors of math on the one side, and a phalanx of supporters (US Department of Education, National Science Foundation, Montgomery County Public Schools) on the other. (By "phalanx" we are not implying any connection to its etymological origins in Greek military organization.)

Not only power relations, but individual self-interest also have to be on the RD table. Both must be distinguished from the fiduciary responsibilities, public acts, and commitments of the US Department of Education (USDOE), for example, whose accountability interests are in those league tables as the outward and visible sign of improvement in math education. The school district's concern is mediation, which, although the result was mixed, was almost an abrogation of its power to outside experts. The parents of the gifted and talented are interested in what they see as the quality of their children's education (like most other people).

Exploring this set of antagonisms so far seems to demand first establishing a context and history of the debate. As we think about similarities and differences between the positions, we need to identify hidden and surrogate problems, then power relations and self-interest.

With that background we can then seek to define more exactly the core of the oppositions, that is the central values and desired outcomes at stake. From the text of the article the two main positions can be characterized in this way:

> Position A. I believe that mathematics is a discipline dedicated to symbolic abstraction and formal proof. Children learning mathematics need sustained practice in computational skills to enable them to work effectively with the processes at the heart of the discipline. I also believe that every child should have the opportunity to learn mathematics. The outcomes have been poor for 85 percent of the nation's children, but this is due to teachers themselves not being acquainted with the discipline.

Position B. I believe that children find the abstraction in mathematics very difficult to comprehend, and they can get deep conceptual understanding of the discipline through working on problems relevant to their lives and to discursive work on their own learning. Many teachers who are not math specialists can therefore provide children with experiences that will help them avoid becoming math-phobic and thereby opening up the opportunity for mathematical progress.

So, what are the similarities? From the article only, it is possible to claim that both sides:

- want children to enjoy mathematics so they are motivated to continue exploring math-related classes and career options;
- believe that children have different talents;
- believe that school children are not being taught math well;
- want children to do well on SATs so they can go to college; and
- want children to have an in-depth understanding of math where they think about what they are doing. And, there may be more.

What are the differences? Certainly, the apparent disagreement on the "nature of math" obscures contrasting approaches to teaching it. Here we have laid out some of the oppositions:

- Group A (the traditional) believes that there is a fixed way to teach it, derived from the character of the discipline. Group B (the Connected Math group) emphasizes that every child can potentially understand mathematics but the approach to it is through individual motivation of the child, not the character of the discipline.
- Notice that most of the children's quotations (and they are surely interested) are about Connected Math. We don't know how the children might stand in regard to differences in their experience. But, they do give some indication that they like this math better than what they have experienced in the past. In this article, their past experiences are not described.
- If the performances and motivations of children are so contrasting, then the gifted and talented parents probably think that the curriculum for some should be not for all, whereas the Connected Math folk believe that "one size fits all." That is, if we figure out a "good" curriculum, every child should do it. Yet that last difference is at the core of the problem as stated.
- The Connected Math people believe that children will be motivated if they understand how math is connected to real-world problems. The traditional people probably believe that children will be motivated if they can learn to enjoy the elegance of math as a logical system (we had to take a leap here since this wasn't stated in the article).
- Both groups want children to have a deep understanding of math. They want them to think about what they are doing. But each group has a

different idea about how to accomplish that goal. From this article, we get the idea that one group thinks it is from drill and practice and focusing on computational skills. The other thinks it is from thinking seriously about how to use math in real-world settings.

What's happening here? We are attempting carefully and gradually to unpack the core conflict, where each group seeks to help the other articulate its view, so that the similarities and differences can be patently clear. Some similarities and differences will be more important than others and we will need to get them ranked in some way because we will need to focus on what is important.

To better understand differences it seems natural to first set aside (for now) those differences on which agreement is unlikely, which echoes Etzioni's (1996) suggestion that some issues be left aside. An easy way to start this process is to isolate the differences in which few have an investment and set them aside. This is difficult to describe from the data of the article. The question of whether children write math journals in either approach might be relatively trivial. A difference could also emerge, we guess, on the character of teacher education for novices and for veterans, involving such questions as specialist teaching, compulsory math courses at different grade-level preparation of teachers.

We have ranked the similarities we outlined on page 30 according to *our* priorities for Jack and Garrett, but of course the advocates involved in this controversy would need to provide their own ranking. But, our rankings are:

1   Want children to enjoy mathematics so they are motivated to continue exploring math-related classes and career options.
2   Want children to have an in-depth understanding of math where they think about what they are doing.
3   Want children to do well on SATs so they can go to college.
4   Believe that children have different talents.
5   Believe that school children are not being taught math well.

Ranking can be a difficult conversation because people will have different priorities. Everyone might agree that children have different talents (which implies nothing about the value of such talents for the moment). They might also agree that children aren't being well taught, but that might be beside the point. We ranked that last because it seemed to us to focus on blame and we believe it is critical in RD to avoid blaming others if a common problem is to be articulated.

In ranking the similarities, we may discover the real differences between the two groups. One group may believe the priority is to motivate children to continue with math (to enjoy math), while the other group may believe it is more important for children to learn math well. We may also find there are differences in the way both groups view motivation. The traditional group might argue that children won't enjoy math until they have struggled with the demands of the discipline, while the Connected Math group would say that's a crazy view of motivation. (But is it?) We now begin to see a product from the discussion. A ranked list of similarities and differences between two apparently fundamental opposed positions is emerging.

Inter-relationships

After establishing similarities, it seems appropriate to examine closely the relationship between the similarities and the differences that were listed. Are some similar aspects from one opposition actually embedded in the other? Are the differences true opposites or simply variations on a common theme? An important first step is to establish common educational practices from the list of similarities. In the Connected Math example, questions of fairness to all children are an obvious moral concern. Aristotle defined equality in a rather interesting way – treat equals equally, but unequals unequally. Scholars think he meant something like this. Where you have people who are the same in the relevant respects, justice demands that you treat them the same. For example, if you are speeding on the highway, it doesn't matter whether you are a doctor or a draftsperson, you are equal as drivers, so you should be treated the same as individuals. With unequals, he was thinking of groups. If you are trying to decide how to teach mathematics to a group of 16-year-old Einsteins, you would be justified on the grounds of fairness to both in doing something different with a group of 16 year olds with Down's syndrome. (This is a good example of how moral thought enlightens and changes perspectives on practice.)

Treating people equally rarely means giving them the same. How might this affect the approach to the problem? The practical issue is what we do. A person could agree to treat children differently in the way they learn mathematics, or in terms of their motivation, but be doing so fairly. At the heart of the differences in practice is a common practical theme – in practice treat all children fairly. From that springs a second common educational practice, namely the determined effort to improve the quality of education in practice.

What seems to have emerged from these centuries of experiment is that children respond to mathematics (as they do to everything else, of course) in hugely varied ways. But it is not sensible, in our view, to think either that most children who study math simply see it as a kind of elaborate chess, or that their parents see it as without any vocational or social purpose. On the other side, having children do practical problems just for the joy of intellectual challenge is not the way Connected Math is designed. It is designed to motivate them through extrinsic rewards. Specifically, learners are taught how math will help them in their everyday interactions. The "drill and kill" methods and Connected Math approach may not seem, from the standpoint of advocates, to have anything of the same pattern. But, from different perspectives on educational purposes, they have one clear similarity: both groups rely on extrinsic motivation. The gifted and talented parents want their children to succeed, get good SAT scores, and go to ivy-league schools. The Connected Math people want their children to succeed, not be math-phobic, maybe get better SAT scores, and maybe go to college unscathed by their experience with mathematics. Out of such a discourse on motivation, we suspect, might also come the realization that people think children should, in some way, come to value mathematics both for its own sake and for its social or vocational purpose.

It is also possible that given a conversation about inter-relationships, advocates would find that the professors of education don't want students to simply engage in drill and practice. The report states that "the Connected Math critics' biggest beef is that although it imbues deep conceptual understanding, it does not teach computation skills." This seems to contradict the idea, presented in the same article, that critics have called Connected Math "fuzzy, or MTV math, or Mickey Mouse Math." It seems more likely that the professors believe Connected Math is not providing a deep conceptual understanding of math and it is not allowing students to practice computational skills. This is a good example of antagonistic discourse polarizing the two groups. One group wants children to think, the other wants them to memorize. With RD, it is possible for groups to have very similar goals, but believe these goals should be achieved in different ways.

Developing a plan for action

The "fundamental, unresolved problem(s)" were stated in the article as "What is math?" And "who gets to learn it?" "How do you teach it?" We might add from our discussions: Should all children have to learn math in the same way? In this analysis, what stands out as possible problems on which both sides can cooperate in RD?

- How do we motivate children to want to learn math?
- How do we teach children math so that they have a deep understanding of math?
- Is there one way to teach math where children think carefully about math, practice computational skills, and connect it to real life?
- Or, perhaps, we could combine these two and ask, "Is there one approach to teaching mathematics suitable for every child that both motivates children to want to learn and helps them to understand math at a deeper level?"

So what might be an appropriate plan of action? Both groups claim to have expertise in an area targeted in our shared problems. The Connected Math people claim to know how to motivate children and to teach children a "deep understanding" of math. The traditional math people claim to know how to teach children how to have a "different kind of deep understanding" of math. At this point, we suggest for people to start the process of RD over, digging even deeper into the details of the debate. It would be important to understand more thoroughly how the Connected Math group "connects" math to real-world problems. The real concerns of the professors need to be better understood. In the Connected Math approach, do children have the chance to practice computation? In the examples provided in the newspaper article, computation was clearly needed so this criticism seems unwarranted from what we read in this article. The article provided us with a few examples of math problems, but not enough to develop a list of similarities or inter-relations that could help us understand the details of the different approaches offered. It would be interesting to know how math professors might suggest that children be taught a deep understanding of math skills. It is hard to believe they would want to use methods that have been proven ineffective for decades. Through RD, we can list similarities and differences in the approaches offered and seek to understand whether people are as polarized as this article suggests. If the groups can agree on a shared problem from our list (or choose another), they should start the process over and continue to work on reconciliation in an attempt to move closer to a solution.

Reflection and speculation

We believe that we have shown provisionally that working at an agreed problem takes entrenched positions into quite new forms of civil discussion with the real possibility of coming to new and alternative public and private judgments. Although the next appropriate course of action in the reconciliatory process would be to select a shared problem and continue the analysis, we can review what we have learned so far and speculate on possible solutions.

First, the differences between these groups do not seem to be associated with underlying goals, but with strategies about how to accomplish those goals. In other words, everyone may agree that children need to learn math better, and that we need to find ways to foster children's interest.

Second, both groups seem satisfied with extrinsic motivation. If they agree on what children should know in math, and how children should be motivated, one possible solution is for both groups to come together and use their expertise to build on the best of both approaches to develop a new approach or to revise the Connected Math approach. If Connected Math does not allow children to practice computation skills, perhaps together the groups could revise the methods to allow more computation practice. This is not the answer for all controversies, but it seems logical in this context. If they do not agree on what children should know in math, the advocates must begin the reconciliation process again with a newly refined problem. The controversy would no longer be about teaching approaches (pedagogy), it would be about what children should know (curriculum).

Third, even from the outside, we can make some progress toward a common problem. In Chapter 1, we claimed that RD aids in developing productive, moral conversations, helps define a problem more accurately, and opens up possibilities for new and better solutions to old, unresolved problems. Even at a very high level of analysis, with limited information, we were able to move forward on these goals.

Indeed, we believe we could articulate a problem both parties share, which could be productive, namely: How can we teach children a deep and meaningful understanding of mathematics that motivates them to continue their studies?

As authors, we asked a question in the introductory chapter. Will Jack and Garrett get from education what we missed? Will they get what we found important? Neither of us liked or understood math much at all, but we would like to see math educators tackling this question in a context of community (Etzioni, 1996), not of antagonism, and also searching seriously world-wide for examples of excellence in math education. This could provide Jack and Garrett with something in their education that was missing in our experience – an in-depth understanding of, and love for, mathematics.

In the next chapter we build on our observations and comments with this example to develop a formal procedure, which might help advocates accomplish this goal through productive conversation.

3 The procedure for RD

With the Connected Math controversy in the previous chapter, we have begun establishing some points of importance in RD that we defined in Chapter 1 in the following way:

> Reconciliatory discourse (RD) is a civil discussion in which participants with divergent views seek to build common ground for (educational) practice through the articulation of a shared problem to which they are all morally and intellectually committed. Participants in RD use compromise, adopt middle ways, and make practical choices to build on the best. They respect divergence and eschew consensus for consensus' sake. They use its principles in writing as well as in practice-oriented discourse. Their purpose is to make better public and private judgments about education.

We now set out a set of mildly formal procedures that people can follow step by step to work through educational controversies. We hope others will try them, see if they work, and alter them for their own experience. We have tried to strike a balance between developing an instrumental approach that can guide people through to action and a moral approach that emphasizes human judgment over rules and procedures. The steps we outline here can be viewed not only as simple rules to follow, but also as representative of habits of mind, of the kind Etzioni described (see p. 13 above), which have been structured into a procedure, a matter we will discuss further in Chapter 5. We begin, however, with the matter of context.

The context for RD

Discourse always takes place in a context, and these are immensely variable in social life. For example, one could imagine RD in such varied contexts as: (a) an after-dinner conversation (or anything similar) where people who have so internalized the basic structure to use it automatically in any general overview of a contested topic, or (b) the production of an article, where a journalist writing a story or a group of researchers is seeking to understand and help others understand the details of a particular controversy.

Four main contexts appeal to us as points of reference:

- family and friends;
- a learning community (e.g., a classroom, church group, or neighborhood watch committee);
- a workplace (e.g., in teams with colleagues, with a boss, or with a subordinate); and
- in the development of public policy (e.g., making decisions about educational policy).

Context is crucial. RD will take different forms, depending on existing animosities or intimacies of the people involved. After-dinner conversations with families or friends often are antagonistic. Where decisions are at a premium, for example a public policy context, emotions and strong argument can run very high. The more at stake, for individuals or institutions, the higher the emotion and the need for the discipline of the discourse. As this will be a new type of discourse for most, the tendency to deploy antagonistic strategies will be great. Therefore we will all need to take careful account of the context in using the procedure. For, while the rudiments of the structure are clear, they will require interpretation for different contexts. In subsequent chapters, we provide examples of RD being used in different ways.

The structure we suggest here seems to us conceptually right. We have started to improve on it by trying it out with groups. At the heart of the endeavor is the articulation of a shared problem.

The definition of a problem

The product of successful reconciliatory discourse (RD) is the understanding of, and authentic acceptance of, the definition of a problem stated with as much clarity as possible. In their book *The New Rational Manager*, Charles Kepner and Ben Tregoe (1997) set out six techniques of problem analysis with a focus on business contexts. Problems arise there because there is a deviation from formerly acceptable performance and a performance that has never quite met expectations. Educators might learn enormously from the Kepner–Tregoe techniques, but business contexts assume agreed ideologies and goals. Educational controversy, as we have described it, can assume no such thing. To repeat our citation of Kepner and Tregoe, "it is important to name the problem precisely because all the work to follow – all the description, analysis, and explanation we will undertake – will be directed at correcting the problem as it has been named" (p. 29).

Exactly.

Yet most educational controversies do not address the same problem, as in the math education debate, because the underlying assumptions, unlike those in business, are different, sometimes dramatically so. Calling something a problem implies that it can be solved. We believe, as we argued with the quick-fix tendency, that we rush to solutions without sufficient discourse about what the problem is. To build on the best, and make an appropriate choice, we need to understand the real problem given the context.

The focus of RD is getting the problem right.

That will be an exercise in collaboration, which can build trust, on the basis of which solutions can be developed. Properly structured, working together to set a problem builds trust. But there is something more to it than merely trust: "Mutual trust is a virtuous circle of anticipation and action whose initiation always requires a leap of faith beyond the available evidence" (Schon and Rein, 1994, p. 179). We have to take risks to trust.

The skeleton of the procedure

As we reflected and wrote drafts of this book, and as we worked through the Connected Math example, we concluded that problem definition had to include at least:

- examining the history of the opposing positions;
- laying out the opposing positions;
- uncovering any hidden problems;
- uncovering any surrogate problems;
- narrowing our focus and naming the issues precisely;
- looking for mutual relationships;
- defining terms;
- agreeing on one question to be answered (prioritizing the problems); and
- identifying similarities and differences between positions.

We broke these down to five basic steps for reconciliatory discourse:

I   Locate the issues.
II   Work out similarities and differences.
III Rank similarities in order of importance.
IV   Establish inter-relationships.
V   Formulate the shared problem.

In this section, we provide a short synopsis of each step in the procedure, before later providing a rationale, description, and importance of each step.

I Locate the issues

People with opposed positions each have a view of their history. They will describe the problem in distinct ways. What, for example, is character educa-tion? What is at stake? Why is it being discussed? Group A might focus on misbehavior, claiming that young people are too promiscuous, using drugs, having sex, and so on. Group B describes the problem in terms of political alienation, the young being turned off politics, not voting, not caring about the wider world. Group C might place the responsibility with the family, advocating character education to offset the breakdown of the family and to provide parenthood education. Faced with these three possibilities, if a person is interested in RD, s/he won't ask "who is right?" S/he will want to describe the location and origins of these different views and why they come from different places. Engaging in RD, a person must have a strong sense of where any controversy is located – historically, socially, and politically.

II Work out similarities and differences

It is possible to then search for similarities and differences. Every position a person takes on a practical problem is influenced not only by personal history, but also by specific political, social, cultural, religious, or moral values. So, once we have the history and the location described, we then need to sort out its central values, its ideology, together with the practices and the outcomes it inspires. Once these are as clear as possible, the contradictory statements of values and the similarities and differences in value and practice must be articulated. The understanding of such contradictory statements, their similarities, and differences constitutes an essential building block in coming to a mutually agreed sense of the problem.

III Rank similarities in order of importance

In principle, out of such an inquiry or conversation could come huge lists of similarities and differences. For the sake of the product defining the problem, everyone must help to clear the decks. This means looking at *differences* first and putting to one side those which either are unlikely to be solved, or no one has any particular investment or interest in. From this everyone will know (a) where the oppositions are, (b) what is central, (c) what is beyond agreement, and (d) what is not viewed as important.

But the key to good problem definition lies in ranking the *similarities*. The list may run right the way from grand statements of value through to a specific practice. For example, imagine a context where a group of teachers and academics are engaged in RD mutually defining a problem on the shape of character education for the third grade. Even though there is widespread agreement on a list of similarities, ranking them may be much more difficult. The practices – what the teacher says, how the class is organized, what is put on the walls, what the books are – will be the more important for teachers. This can also be done with purely theoretical issues too: for example, in establishing views of truth and meaning in Aristotle, John Stuart Mill, and John Dewey, the extent of similarities and differences, and ranking the importance of those similarities and differences.

We repeat the importance of context. We can't describe the similar values over here and similar practices over there. Practices cannot be fully described without explicit description of the values that support them. For similarities are important only to a context, in this case a third-grade curriculum. The context needs to be described. Ranking similarities therefore also functions as a check on whether the similarities are what they appear to be. Ranking provides for evaluation of an agenda. It may well result in retracing one's steps to understand the similarities once again.

IV Establish inter-relationships

This is the step in the procedure where we seek common ground. We've got the historical and contemporary oppositions in our heads, and we have not only worked through similarities and differences, but also ranked them, suggesting what is critically important as we approach problem definition.

The category of inter-relations has two dimensions. First, we explore what people do in practice. Ignoring practical realities is one of the main reasons that good ideas in education fail. Second, we explore how oppositions are inter-related (e.g., how they are dependent on each other or embedded within one another). In this category, we seek to understand how oppositions relate to each other, especially given the realities of what actually happens in classrooms, as opposed to what is supposed to happen in classrooms.

This is also a point at which a reality check is needed. We can't properly figure out the inter-relationships of *what people do*, the practice of teaching and learning in its widest sense, without evidence of some kind. What do people do in character education lessons? How do teachers on the job teach children to be honest? How can the conversation be widened to describe inter-relationships without, for example, some exploration of the nature of deceit, the power plays that involves, and the connection of truth to language?

In order to understand what happens in practice, it is important to support claims with evidence, such as teacher research studies. Remember that the purpose of looking at the evidence is not to "find the best approach," but to explore whether the similarities we have uncovered provide instances of practical inter-relationships and mutual dependencies. Once again, this will provide opportunities for back tracking, for revising conclusions reached at earlier stages. It will also convince the participants that the common ground they are on is real and is firm.

V Formulate the shared problem

From such disciplined discourse, the problem will readily emerge in language that contains profound mutual understandings. It is on that basis that solutions to problems can be found. Solutions are indelibly linked to actual contexts. Finding solutions is, for us, a distinct form of practical discourse requiring a new book. Kepner and Tregoe (1997) have a tried and tested procedure in business. Schon and Rein (1994) use their experience in design to describe a strategy for coming to solutions.

The procedure for RD

On these five basic elements in the structure we can now build and explain an extended and detailed RD procedure. The new elements are designed to help us to achieve the goal – the definition of a mutually agreed problem that represents a reconciliation of different aims. In this section, we further describe each step of the procedure, and we provide a rationale for each of the steps. It should be emphasized that the character of RD can only be tested through contexts and conversations.

The procedure

I   **Locate the issues**
(a)   Describe the oppositions and their origins.
(b)   Identify any hidden issues.
(c)   Identify any surrogate problems.

     Product: Description of real oppositions.

II   **Work out similarities and differences**
(a)   Revisit the conditions and requirements for participants.
(b)   Suspend judgment.
(c)   Describe self-interests and participant power relations.
(d)   Set out central values and outcomes.
(e)   Identify perceived similarities and differences.

     Product: The initial agenda of similarities and differences.

III   **Rank similarities in order of importance**
(a)   Examine the progress of the discourse.
(b)   Work out those differences on which agreement is unlikely.
(c)   Isolate the differences in which few have an investment and set them aside.
(d)   Rank the similarities in order of importance.

     Product: The developed agenda of differences and similarities.

IV   **Establish inter-relationships**
(a)   Establish common educational practices from the list of similarities.
(b)   Define mutual interdependencies of similar practices.

V   **Formulate the shared problem**
(a)   Define the problem.
(b)   Review each product and develop a plan of action.

     Product: Full statement of the problem with an agreed agenda for action.

I Locate the issues

(a) Describe the oppositions and their origins

Using the character education example, we indicated the importance of determining the history of an issue. People with opposed positions each have a view of their history, so they describe the problem in distinct ways. The first step in the process of locating the issues is to place it historically as well as in its contemporary context. The character education example suggests that two of the positions (misbehavior and family) could stem from a religious position whereas the other (political alienation) suggests a civic and secular orientation to community and society. This immediately raises the familiar tension between church and state in matters of moral behavior that will form a central part of the discourse. It raises also issues of responsibility among institutions, church, school, and family. The differences in diagnosis of the need for character education spread out beyond the classroom.

(b) Identify any hidden issues

Sometimes in discussions, people play their cards close to the chest (note the competitive metaphor!) and the real issue on one or the other side is not revealed. This is different from diplomatic or political discussions where one or other party may have no true interest in solving the problem, but is using the time to stall actions elsewhere.

How can issues get hidden in RD? A simple example. Your daughter's teacher advises her and you to have her take AP Government. Your child wants to do French, and you support her. The teacher gets more and more adamant about French being a poor choice. The disagreement could arise because the teacher's real problem is not being disclosed to you. For example, the teacher is an AP Government teacher and the enrolments aren't good (which is the real problem!). Or, the teacher knows the (unmarried) French teacher (whom your child adores) is pregnant and likely to leave. The teacher can't tell you because she knows the French teacher is considering all her options, from abortion to marrying the father, and she has been sworn to secrecy anyway (which is the real problem!). So the teacher is really trying not so much to get your child to do AP Government as to avoid the choice of French and then be let down. Or, of course, you might be disguising the real problem, namely that you and your child think the French teacher is much more hardworking, much less committed to grammar tests than to enjoying Balzac, while the AP Government teacher–adviser is test driven for success, which you don't like.

This simple example carries an important lesson. Unless people declare themselves, they can't build trust (but see page 28 on self-interest). The adviser with a personal confidence about the French teacher could easily say "I can't disclose what the real problem is here: it's private." That is far better than concealing it.

Your dislike of test-driven teaching can be stated too, but you have to be aware of the moral situation and impact an outright declaration might have.

(c) Identify any surrogate problems

How often have we been in a discussion when someone has said "You know, we are meant to be discussing X here, but I think the real problem is Y"? And participants then argue about whether that is the problem or not. We know too from our personal lives how we use "surrogate topics." Pam argues with Dave, or Hugh argues with Ann, about the color of the paint for the bathroom. But this argument is a surrogate for our real disagreement on whether to spend money on painting the room at all. We define a surrogate topic as one that appears to be a source of conflict but is simply taking the place of the real issue. It behooves every participant to ensure that is not the case.

We now have a product, in fact three things of importance. First, the broad outlines of the oppositions in a particular controversy have been sketched and mutually understood. Second, hidden or surrogate problems have been revealed. Third, the collaboration required is building the trust needed for the complex issues ahead.

II Work out similarities and differences

Once a problem is established and agreed, the quality of the discussion is dependent on a mutual search for the similarities and differences, both on practice and on values.

(a) Revisit the conditions and requirements for participants

At this point in the procedure it is necessary first to conduct a review and a brief evaluation of the process. In Chapter 5, we will talk about specific conditions and requirements for participation in RD that will help guide this process. Critical to this part of the procedure is the clear identification of how individual people, their perspectives, interests, and status, interact with the statement of their ideology and how dependent practices are understood.

(b) Suspend judgment

We have all been in situations where someone, perhaps inadvertently, makes a comment that makes us stereotype the person as, say, a racist or a sexist; witness the 1998 report of the Public Agenda Foundation (*A Lot to Be Thankful For*). People's prejudices are often not confirmed by the facts, so we need a way of putting our prejudices on one side and suspending judgment.

This may seem impossible, but in practice there are various devices to be tried. First and foremost, suspension of judgment means a special type of listening. It demands a kind of internal conversation which is more like "am I fully understanding what is being said?" rather than "how can I show this guy he is wrong, or racist, or sexist?" Second, suspension of judgment can be practically assisted by a participant who does not sympathize with a particular position being asked to articulate it. This is an important way of being able to see a position from the inside, and, in so doing, suspending judgment. The British historian R. G. Collingwood (1946) argued that the only way we could understand historical characters, like George Washington, was to try to imagine what it was like to see the world from their point of view, indeed to recapitulate their thinking. Finally, suspension of judgment requires that a person stand at some distance from her/his own position, as if it were someone else's.

(c) Describe self-interests and participant power relations

Not everything has to be on the table in reconciliatory discourse, but it is important to know where people's self-interests lie and what are the power relations among the participants.

To propose the elaboration of self-interest is not to criticize putative participants. We all have varying degrees of self-interest and individual perspective, or we wouldn't be engaging in the discourse. We believe that declarations of self-interest and individual perspective can assist in the delineation of the similarities and differences of the positions and in people gleaning a broader understanding of the context of the problem.

For example, say you are a teacher who is interested in developing an after-school computer program and you are talking with a superintendent. The superintendent's *individual perspective* will mean s/he will certainly want to know how the program will benefit the children, and will also be interested in the cost and in issues of personnel. If the superintendent has shares in the company providing the program, then s/he has a self-interest, and, so that trust can continue to be built, s/he should declare that. If you are talking with a parent, the parent will self-interestedly want to know how this program will benefit her/his child, but probably won't care about the cost or who plans to staff the center. As you talk to different participants, their self-interests will emerge as well as your own. We believe that this step in the procedure also enables us to revisit any hidden problems.

Sometimes self-interest can be appropriate and useful but at other times not. Parents handling sibling rivalries know that they are teaching children to be less self-interested and oriented toward another. Jack's parents, Victoria and Greg, have been teaching him and his younger sister Hanna to share toys and other things. Jack particularly has to be helped to cope with his jealousies about his parents' attention with his sister. On this basis he will build his understanding of what it is to consider the needs of others and from which he will distinguish those things which are in his self-interest. Pamela and David, on the other hand, must be very careful with Garrett (who is still an only child) that he doesn't grow up believing he does not need to consider the needs of others. Some people have simply been raised improperly and feel entitled to certain privileges. A balanced view of our self-interest is also critical as the basis of the commitment to civic fairness.

Self-interest is not helped by self-effacement, a kind of "my interests don't matter." Hugh's mother Dorothy was famous in the family because, if she was offered a chair, she would ask which you preferred before sitting down; or if she were offered a cookie, she would ask which one you wanted before making her choice. For her, it was always someone else's turn! Fortunately, she was not like that in stating her point of view. Yet had she been, it would have been difficult to conduct a reconciliatory discourse with her for you wouldn't have known whether she had genuinely reconciled a point of view or was just being, as she saw it, polite and self-effacing.

Self-interest can be problematic when differential power relations allow for one person with power to have her/his way. In some ways we have written about reconciliatory discourse as if each individual within a conversation *always* has equal status. We recognize this is not true, although to have a reconciliatory discussion, both sides must try to interact within the conversation as if they are equal. When a teacher talks to a parent or a parent talks to a teacher or a superintendent talks to a teacher or a teacher talks to a college professor, in each situation the power relations are different.

In our view, the key way in which power is redistributed in RD is when participants all take the conditions and requirements *seriously* – hence our suggestion that they be revisited. Each participant must attend to the commitments and requirements in a different way according to their status. Those with a higher status need to be committed to listening more intently to others. Beyond listening, they need to value diverse perspectives and know they can learn from those who are younger, less experienced, or less knowledgeable. Those who have a lower status (for whatever reason) must attend to feelings of inadequacy, resentment, frustration, hero worship, or whatever comes from a lesser status. In differential power relationships we cannot always judge how the other person is going to respond because we cannot always predict how they feel as a result of their status. As a young assistant professor, Pamela is surprised that occasionally she will come across experienced, full professors who seem insecure about their abilities. In most situations, when interacting with senior faculty, Pamela would attend to her lower status, but in some rare cases this assumption is wrong and she must adapt her strategies for interaction. Differential power relations will certainly affect your reconciliatory process. The task is to ensure they don't damage it.

Once self-interest and power relations are on the table, the playing field has been leveled, at least in principle, for discussion of values.

(d) Set out central values and outcomes

When we located the issues, we got a general map. Now we need to articulate the opposed positions. The basis of trust being established now receives its first major test. For the task here is not merely for individuals to lay out their positions, but for the development of those positions to be seen as *mutual tasks, not one where individuals have to "state and defend."*

Let's explain. From the definition of the problem, we have built patterns of trust and collaboration and we have a product we have celebrated. So far, too, we have set out our self-interests, individual perspectives, and understood power relations that exist in most groups. Now each participant takes the problem as now defined and sets out her/his general values. For example, if character education was under discussion, a participant might say:

> I am a Roman Catholic. For me, monogamy is a matter of God's will, marriage a holy sacrament and children God's gift. Children must be brought up to love God and his laws with the family, and the school in concert with the family and the church, playing the central role. The child's character is therefore rooted in a moral conscience driven by Catholic religious values.

Another participant might say:

> I am first and foremost an individual citizen. For me, life, liberty and the pursuit of happiness are the ultimate values which imply respect for others and consideration of the interests of others, both as individuals and citizens. How children eventually choose to live their life is a matter of their choice, but they must acquire the habits of good citizenship, including volunteerism and philanthropy.

Crucial in the interests of RD is that the articulation of individual values be well prepared. However, these statements are not just left on the table. They require detailed inquiry and follow-up by all participants. It then becomes a *group task* to fill out the central values and the outcomes that can be claimed to emerge from such value statements or ideologies. For example, how is family defined? Does it mean only natural parents? What are the rights and duties of citizens? Every participant sees it as her/his task to help the individual citizen articulate with maximum clarity, say, what might be the citizen's responsibilities to others, or, to help the Roman Catholic to describe the value of the family, school, and church working together.

Mutual inquiry must be robust. There is a tendency for groups struggling with trust to work toward consensus so as not to rock the boat. This is a mistake at this stage, for consensus will leave all kinds of problems dangling in the conversation. To ensure understanding, different positions need to be starkly stated. There is another weakness in having a group of individuals take turns stating their views. If there are a dozen people sitting round, answering questions in turn, the odds are very high that by the time the questions reach the twelfth person, that person will claim that what s/he wants to say has already been said. This part of the procedure therefore demands that people be able to seek out and assert their divergence. This is the positive side of the suspension of judgment. In antagonistic debate, someone might say to the individual citizen "well, you just believe in people doing whatever they want" or to the Catholic "you just want to impose your God on everyone else." In reconciliatory form, the articulation is not a forensic challenge, but a mutual search for understanding.

(e) Identify perceived similarities and differences

Merging into, but not co-extensive with, statements of values is the articulation of similarities and differences. We believe our experience of collaboration is interesting and relevant here. For it is in this step that the difficulty of trust building becomes very pronounced. Similarities and differences have to be collaboratively described, for collaboration is a type of reconciliation. In the best scenario, two people can work together and build on the best. In the worst scenario, two people can work together and not only make each other miserable, but actually create a product that is worse than what they could have produced on their own. What did we do?

First, we worked to develop a common understanding and a shared sense of meaning. What did Pamela mean by reconciliation? What aims of education were important to Hugh? How did we work to reconcile aims in our own practice? When did we agree? When did we disagree? What was at the heart of what seemed like jumbled random thoughts? We realized early that we were after reconciliation, but that meant we had to understand how we were similar and how we were different.

We were constantly asking ourselves what was important? What were we trying to communicate? What did we both want to accomplish? We spent time reflecting on the process. By the end of the collaboration, we were dependent on each other to provide feedback. The weaknesses of each of us were complemented by the strengths of the other, but each of us was able to help the other articulate what s/he wanted to say. It is possible that when we first met, we could have dismissed the idea of working together as impossible. Hugh could have dismissed Pamela as a young, navel-gazing, blonde. Pamela could have written Hugh off as one of those elite, dead-white-guy-worshipping, Brits. Beyond the stereotypes we learned to listen to each other. Once we did that, we realized we had something to learn from each other. While trying to develop a formal process for reconciliation, we didn't have one to use. Like other people, we fumbled along hoping that by the end, we didn't hate each other.

What does this experience tell us about the identification of perceived similarities and differences, following statements of value? Go for the similarities first! Once again (and you must be getting quite bored with us saying this, even though it deserves repetition), the challenge is to build trust as a part of reconciliation, but also to build into the process action patterns that will aid, not undermine, that process. So if people start by describing the differences, rather than the similarities, they are going to be in a defensive mood by the time *their* differences are described. But these differences need to be stated, so it is critical that they are very public, not swept under any carpet.

Remember this is a mutual task. What can the Roman Catholic and the individual citizen describe as their similarities? One obvious building block is a profound respect for human life and for the individual, even though one sees human life in religious and the other in secular terms. What could each of them pick out as a similarity in the other's position with their own? The whole (discussion) is more than the sum of its parts. All can teach and all can learn, as our colleague and friend Todd Endo constantly reiterates. It is the complementariness of participants in RD that can lead to agreed statements of differences and similarities.

Once again we have a product: the description of values and outcomes as a mutual enterprise will have produced a very large list of similarities and differences. Perhaps more important has been the struggle to suspend judgment and the confidence in participants that will have been raised by the enunciation of self-interest and power relations.

III Rank similarities in order of importance

We now need to clear the decks and focus. In the previous section on similarities, we described the importance of examining values and practices together in a context. We demonstrated how listing similarities provided an opportunity to check agreements and understanding and to evaluate the agenda. We need now to engage in redefining the problem through selecting the really important matters from the list of similarities and differences. This is a relatively short, but critically important, stage as it enables us to prioritize the problem agenda.

Although we have stated this as "clearing the decks" we are in fact trying to:

- determine the level of importance of similarities and to come up with a prioritized list; and
- put to one side those differences which are either unlikely to be solved, or no one has any particular investment or interest in.

From these we will know where the discussion is, what is central, what is beyond agreement, and what is viewed as unimportant.

(a) Examine the progress of the discourse

Reflecting on and evaluating the progress of the discourse seems to us essential. Do the products so far accurately represent what people have said? Has the process worked for everyone? Is anyone being shut out? If so, why? This continues to build trust.

(b) Work out those differences on which agreement is unlikely

We have moved through the process, emphasizing similarities as critical to reconciliation. While the focus in the previous step has been on similarities, this is on differences. If the list of differences is quite short, it can be constructed as a rank order of importance to participants. Some may be too crucial to ignore and they have to be kept in mind. Others may be insignificant and can be set aside. The task is to establish those irreconcilable differences that do not overwhelm the similarities.

However, the differences may mean that the discourse should stop. That is, the list of differences may far exceed the established similarities. In other words, not much potential for reconciliation seems to exist. In that event, participants need to review their differences in what Schon and Rein (1994) would call a different frame. "Okay, we differ on this and that, but could we examine it from a different viewpoint?" Take the character education example again. The value positions as stated were quite general. Say people can't detect similarities. What if both sides considered something unusual, say the moral education of a 16-year-old Ukrainian Muslim non-English-speaking immigrant? Which concepts would we want him to understand first? Would that reframe the discourse?

That may fail. The differences (and the personalities) may just be too profound. It may well be that between the evolutionist and the literal creationist (see Chapter 8), or between the Roman Catholic and the non-religious citizen, there is just too great a gulf. Does the experience of discourse so far indicate a promise of reconciliation? If not, halt the process.

(c) Isolate the differences in which few have an investment and set them aside

Once the list of differences is established and judgment made about their significance, some of them may be thought unimportant or uninteresting to those taking part. They need to be removed from the revised agenda.

(d) Rank the similarities in order of importance

We can then get to the product list of similarities, having understood where the differences lie. Similarities are the focus of RD, because they are the basis for the formulation of the agreed problem. We showed early that ranking is critical because of other differences (e.g., between third-grade teachers and academics), which displayed priorities not so far visible in the discourse. Remember that every participant and every discussion are context bound, and that values and practices must be ranked.

Yet for us, the great value for the purposes of reconciliation in ranking the values is that each voice counts for one and none for more than one. This is the opportunity where, whatever system is used, participants are on a level playing field. For the fact is that, however solicitous participants may be to ensure that every voice is heard, the dynamic of conversation is not always toward the reconciliator, the listener, the thoughtful, the search for mutual understanding, and those other characteristics we would like to see. Ranking should be publicly displayed to reveal persisting differences and unrecognized similarities.

The product is now a developed agenda of important similarities. This agenda will now begin to prove its utility in two ways. First, it can now look like an agenda which, given further work, will provide the concepts and the ideas for problem definition. Second, it should now be an agenda that gets at mutual understanding of the core of the oppositions, but which can still be deepened and become more searching to get the problem agreed. That can't be determined until the final step.

Of course, no product will be available if differences have proved too intractable.

IV Establish inter-relationships

This is the step where, we believe, the art of RD is at its zenith. The product will be the definition of a problem, representing common ground among oppositions, and providing an agenda for action. So far we have:

- worked on the similarities and differences in any set of oppositions; and
- cleared the decks somewhat by agreeing on important similarities or agreeing that our differences are irreconcilable.

We now need to look at what the common ground looks like. As we indicated in Chapter 1, reconciliation can be a matter of compromise, of taking a centrist view, of integrating positions to establish common ground. In this category, we seek to understand what is common in practice and how our different positions are related, which could include how they are dependent on each other or actually embedded within one another.

(a) Establish common educational practices from the list of similarities

RD in education is about *what people do*. For example, education specialists constantly argue that children should learn to be intrinsically motivated to do well in school. It is thought that we should seek to instill a love of learning in children that will carry them through their lifetimes. Educators frequently denounce extrinsic rewards. Yet extrinsic rewards such as stickers, candy, and extra free time are commonplace in the classroom. So, although both groups agree that children should be intrinsically motivated, the shared problem is embedded in the realities of practice, not in the shared philosophy of what should happen. As we seek to understand the practical inter-relations, it is about the practice of teaching and learning in its widest sense. Nothing is more inhibiting to RD than avoiding what happens in practice. What do people do in character education lessons? How do teachers teach children to be honest? We can all rant on about the value and importance of honesty, but how is it tackled in classrooms where children come from diverse backgrounds including those where it is not a particular virtue? But equally, discussion about practice can be sterile without profound consideration of the value positions that are embedded in it. It is not enough to say "Well, we should all be honest, shouldn't we?" without some exploration of the nature of deceit, the power plays that involves, and the connection of truth to language; that is, the practical ramifications of the principle.

Get evidence of practices for review. It is never enough, in our view, to have a person report on practice, for all of us embellish (or detract from) our own experience. Discussion should be prompted by evidence, in whatever form is appropriate, ranging from student evaluations to videotape, from teacher reports or research to parent descriptions. Evidence from teachers' research is increasingly available and helpful. For this can be shared, not be merely the statements of experts.

Zoborfsky and Hauser (1996) are two teachers who studied with us. They believed that forms of testing were tedious and uninformative with their children in fifth and sixth grade from a suburban middle-class school. Therefore, they asked the parents (through a series of reconciliatory discussions, it should be noted) if they would approve these students being asked to demonstrate in ways of their own choosing that they knew particular concepts. In their report of this work, they provide some wonderful examples of the ingenuity with which children showed themselves not merely knowledgeable but accountable. Their discussions with parents revealed two main things: (a) that parents disliked standardized testing intensely and (b) that they constantly underestimated their children's abilities, as seen in the surprise with which they greeted their children's interpretations. Teacher Research Reports like this, especially those that display children's work, are immensely powerful and important accounts of practice. For, of course, it is the quality of children's work that matters above all else.

If the agenda of similarities has been effectively arrived at, then examining evidence of practice will entrench the similarities, or, of course, remind one of differences. The purpose of looking at the evidence is, once again, not to "find the best" at this stage, but to ensure that by checking the agenda of formal similarities against evidence, the common ground the participants think they are on is real and is firm. Without looking at evidence together, different images of practice can be projected.

(b) Define mutual interdependencies of similar practices

If a person finds two opposed positions with similar practices, what is the character of their interdependence?

Failure to notice mutual dependencies is a feature of polarization. We often found that oppositions we studied in writing this book were not as oppositional as they had been advertised. It was common for arguments on both sides to be polarized way out of proportion with reality. That can happen even where we think similarities have been agreed. For example, what may not have emerged in a discussion between phonics and whole language advocates would be their views of the child. That prompts query as to whether they hold related views of learning, what is common about their views of language and culture and how are they related in foreign language acquisition, or the language of mathematics.

Getting at the practical inter-relationships, therefore, demands practical examples, visual if possible and certainly including the work of children. Illustrations of the practice can reveal how apparently opposed practices are mutually interdependent.

Here is another example of mutual dependency. One serious opposition running through education is whether children should be taught to compete or to cooperate (see Chapter 4). That breaks out into all kinds of issues, cheating, training for society, competition for jobs or teamwork within them, and so on. Yet in order to compete one must have cooperation. (Anyone who has played any competitive game knows how irksome it is when one person wants to compete and the other won't cooperate in the competition.) Watch the Super Bowl as a paradigm of competition, yet watch too how the government of the game by rules yields intense cooperation between the sides and it is a spirit that is absolutely vital to the game.

Look at what is done, not just what people say! Results can be surprising. In moral education, the view of individual autonomy held by the individual citizen may be articulated as free will in the Catholic concept of character education. Some contemporary views of "liberal" education depend on vocationally valuable outcomes. Generally, we think people will have a much easier time finding connections and dependencies between apparent opposites than the proponents of either extreme would have us believe, especially if we look at the mutual dependencies that arise from practice.

V Formulate the shared problem

(a) Define the problem

Notice there is only one problem to specify – at any rate for the purposes of RD. Remember, this discussion is about how to name the problem, not to solve it. We believe the following guidelines will be valuable:

- State the problem as a question.
- Keep the question short.
- Never state the question as an either–or.

Stating the problem as a question has the effect of forcing participants to reflect and to go back to basic positions from which they may find more agreement than they suspect, whereas an affirmative statement "The Problem IS ..." will sound accusatory.

The problem should be short, so that it is easy to handle.

The problem should never be an either–or, because that promotes a competitive framework immediately. There is no way we have found to state an either–or question on practical or values matters that does not imply a conflict.

Moreover, such questions are extremely difficult to phrase in a way that is fair to each side. Stating the questions as either–or will needlessly complicate the discussion.

(b) Review each product and develop a plan of action

The product is that the problem is named.

The full procedure will have three interlocking products so far: the description of the real oppositions, the initial agenda, and the developed agenda of similarities and differences. From these five major steps, each with its constitutive procedures, comes a product – the full final statement of the problem with a supporting agenda of similarities enhanced by practical evidence.

We now have three options:

- move toward a solution to the problem because we have established common ground; or
- re-examine the steps, because an articulated agreement seems unreachable; or
- break off the conversation because, for all our best efforts, new differences have emerged to sink a mutual agreement.

The choices are clear enough. Our expectation is that if participants have gotten through to this stage, they will have established sufficient common ground, though they may have, in their list of differences, a further set of problems which a repeat cycle will enhance. We don't believe that the moral and intellectual energy used will often result in a decision to stop talking.

The anticipated outcomes

Apart from these five products, what do we anticipate will be the outcomes of this procedure?

Participants from different outlooks will have

- built common ground from divergent positions, embodied in a shared definition of a problem to solve;
- built a basis of trust, especially in terms of declaring self-interest and power-relationships;
- developed personal moral and intellectual skills including:
  1 the ability to suspend judgment,
  2 the ability to get inside the views of an opponent,
  3 the skill of attending to evidence, and
  4 the ability to make decisions on the basis of importance;
- developed the disciplines of the discourse;
- built a framework for understanding the examination of the quality of discourse in a democratic society; and

- developed a commitment to continue the process in other contexts, for example writing research, working with children or teachers or any group in which there are implicit or explicit oppositions.

The way forward

In Chapter 4 we take the procedure and use it to reconcile the controversy between competition and collaboration. In Chapter 5, we describe the conditions for participants that must be met to eliminate barriers to effective RD. In Chapters 6, 7, and 8 we take one major educational topic per chapter and examine it either as an overview of a field or as a particular controversy. Armed with these examples for procedure and content, we believe that the process has wide applicability.

4 How should children learn?

Competition and collaboration

In this chapter we take the framework of our procedure and apply it to competition and collaboration with respect to children learning. We work broadly to reconcile these oppositions. We are thus not trying to get as close to real life as advocates would, as we did with the math education example in Chapter 2. Rather we use the procedure here by carefully following the five main categories, but using the sub-categories only when needed, sometimes collapsing two steps into one.

The RD procedure is designed for conversation, not written analysis of this kind, but the analysis will demonstrate its applicability. Procedural steps like suspending judgment and declaring power relations are unnecessary in a written example. Another distinction between written and conversational RD is that written RD will be grounded in ideology and theory, while conversational RD will be grounded in practical resolution. Also, as we mentioned before, we are not interested in simply providing a recipe, we want the RD procedures to be adapted to a given context. Finally, we provide a loose structure as we focus on broader conflicts. We believe that the RD procedures can help people with broad, seemingly unsolvable problems find ways to continue narrowing and redefining their problems, providing a clear picture of the true nature of the conflict.

Our thoughts on competition and collaboration were greatly influenced by our experience writing this book. Our collaborative efforts were both enjoyable and productive. The collaboration we experienced allowed us to transcend our own limitations and move beyond old ways of thinking. On the other hand, the first draft of this chapter was written on a holiday, a day when both of us were at home juggling work and family. Hugh worked while waiting for out-of-town guests. Pamela stole moments while Garrett napped or watched his favorite TV show. We quickly e-mailed our ideas back and forth. While collaboration allowed us to present better arguments, part of what propelled us forward on a holiday certainly was influenced by a need to present ideas in a competitive academic climate. This is not to say that we had to finish that day or we would lose our jobs: it was much more complex. Whether illusion or reality, there was a feeling that to stop would mean to lose. We would lose our momentum; we would lose our enthusiasm; we might never finish our book. Even between the two of us (people supposedly enlightened about these issues) there exists a deeply ingrained compulsion to compete. Would we be as motivated if we had no such compulsion? Would we be motivated simply by the enjoyment of the activity and the desire to share our thoughts? Would we take more time to learn and to develop better arguments if collaboration was valued above the competitive reward structure inherent in the final product? These are some of the many deep questions embedded in competition and collaboration. In the introductory chapter, we asked whether Jack and Garrett would get what we missed from education. Would they get what we thought important? The competition and collaboration opposition poses yet another question. What type of adults do we want Garrett and Jack to become? Two men who are driven by their compulsion to compete? Two men who enjoy learning from others? Both? Neither? Nel Noddings (1997) vehemently argues that the primary aim of education should be to produce competent, caring, loving, and lovable people. She refers to this as a morally defensible mission for the schools in the twenty-first century.

In this chapter, we don't plan to explore the competitive nature of a capitalistic economic system or the competitive nature of sports. We realize, of course, the complexity of inter-relations between a society's economic structure and its education system. We focus on (a) the choices that teachers make daily about whether to set up competitive reward structures and activities in K–12 (kindergarten to twelfth grade) classrooms, and (b) the nature of competition in education and its association with sorting and classifying students. It is acknowledged, however, that this controversy is greatly influenced by the competitive nature of our society.

I Locate the issues

Describe the oppositions and their origins

Writers tried to convince us to use collaborative strategies as opposed to competitive strategies. The evidence used to persuade us often pointed to traditional research studies. In fact, David and Roger Johnson, two brothers involved in psychological research, tell us that since 1889 over 500 experimental and 100 correlational research studies have been conducted on cooperative, competitive, and individualistic educational efforts (see Johnson and Johnson, 1989, for a complete review of these studies). Much of the literature suggests that cooperation or collaboration is the answer to a number of classroom ills from boredom, to improper discipline, to ineffective learning. The fact that competition versus collaboration still elicits major controversy speaks to the fact that research studies have not convinced people to change their opinions or their values.

Defining competition

Competition is hard to define. In their book about competition in education, Rich and DeVitis (1992) present three conditions that lay the foundation for competition. They claim that to compete we need two or more persons or groups striving for a reward. The reward needs to be in short supply and only a limited number of persons have access to it. And finally, how people work to gain the reward is rule governed. The last point is quite important because, later, we will discuss the fact that competition has a bad reputation, not always from competition itself, but for different reasons associated with the rules. People often criticize the ill effects of competition both in society and in education, but proponents of competition, like Rich and DeVitis (1992), claim that it has a number of beneficial functions. They say it can:

- encourage a person to make use of her/his full abilities;
- encourage people to reach for high standards;
- help to ensure that benefits and burdens are fairly allocated to the general public;
- protect the public from unfair economic conditions and incompetent public officials;
- help us develop better qualified educators;
- help promote learning; and
- stimulate advancement in science, education, and other fields.

Defining collaboration

The literature on collaborative learning has its roots in the psychological foundations of teaching and learning. If a K–12 teacher takes a college course in psychological foundations of education or in teaching methods, s/he will certainly be exposed to cooperative learning strategies and the theories behind social learning.

The Johnson brothers (1994) provide a description of what they call the theoretical underpinnings for cooperative learning. They claim there are at least three general theoretical perspectives that have guided research on cooperative learning in the last 100 years. Social interdependence theory assumes that cooperative efforts are based on intrinsic motivation generated by the enjoyment people experience while working together to accomplish a significant goal. This theory focuses on relationship issues that crop up when people work together (group dynamics), not what happens to each individual person (personal psychology). The behavioral–social perspective assumes that cooperative efforts are influenced by extrinsic motivation to achieve group rewards. The cognitive–developmental perspective is based on the idea that interaction helps people to learn because when people interact, their thought patterns change. Differences among the perspectives have created conflicts and disagreements that have not been resolved. One of the reasons there are so many research studies on cooperative learning is because academics have generated a considerable body of research to confirm or disprove hypotheses associated with these (and many other) theoretical perspectives.

The cognitive–developmental perspective in large part is based on the theories of Jean Piaget (1954) and Lev Vygotsky (1986). Piaget believed that when people cooperate, they engage in conversations that create cognitive conflicts that need to be resolved. During that time inadequate reasoning is exposed and modified. Vygotsky believed that knowledge is socially constructed from cooperative efforts to learn, understand, and solve problems. Group members exchange information and insights, discover weak points in each other's reasoning strategies, correct one another, and adjust their understanding on the basis of other people's understanding.

The difference between cooperation and collaboration is basically that cooperative learning is an extension of peer collaboration but more formal and structured. Cooperative learning demands careful and continuous monitoring, processing, and assessment by the instructor if it is to be worthwhile.

Cooperation/competition and fairness

Experts tell us that we can use cooperative groups to produce successful learning (Johnson and Johnson, 1994; Cohen, 1994; Slavin, 1990). Professor Elizabeth Cohen (1994) of Stanford University claims that group work can help children learn because dialogue helps move them forward in logical thinking. It can help children understand concepts as when one student is helping another analyze sentence structures. It helps children understand and retain information and it aids in the learning of language. It also has positive effects on how people feel about each other (social goals) and it helps bring children together in classrooms segregated by race, class, and gender. It has a positive effect of socializing students for adult roles. When students cooperate, they learn how to be active citizens (in a collective, rather than individualistic, sense). It also assists the teacher in addressing behavior problems.

Competition is thought of differently. Although we constantly compete physically, mentally, and monetarily, competition is often criticized. Most of the criticisms point to the fact that in competitive societies, when one person is on the top, another is on the bottom. At the bottom we find the disaffected, the disenchanted, and the disloyal. Those who argue competition is harmful believe that cooperation should be valued over competition because in practice people don't have equal opportunity to compete for rewards (Rich and DeVitis, 1992). For example, it has been argued that what is valued in a competition is determined by the ruling class (Banks, 1986). In our society, older white males have power. Therefore, what these men think is important, and more importantly what they are good at, determines the competition. It is conceivable this is one reason the ability to argue aggressively is valued and antagonistic debate is considered normal. If there were more elected women officials, perhaps empathic cognition and care would be valued more highly.

With regard to competition, many believe they do not have a fair chance to compete because of their race, class, or gender. Background and other variables affect whether people are more or less interested or skilled in competition. In a previous research study, Pamela found that highly successful women from disadvantaged backgrounds claimed they liked competition, but not in the way that it was most often defined. These women liked competing against themselves. According to her research, the women never did care whether others did well; in fact many felt bad when fellow students did poorly. They didn't care what other children were doing, they concentrated on competing against themselves and challenging themselves to do better (LePage-Lees, 1997).

The issue of fairness is addressed in a number of examples of non-competitive theories of education including Rousseau's romanticism, Dewey's progressivism, libertarianism, Marxism, and feminism. Most of these theories emphasize student freedom (or more accurately the absence of coercion or restriction) and non-authoritarian rule. They value teacher friendliness above control, enthusiasm rather than obedience, and cooperation rather than competition. Many talk about educating the whole child, questioning the dominant paradigms and emphasizing issues of equity (Rich and DeVitis, 1992).

Issues of inequity provide one example of why people think competition is harmful. Others argue that competition in education can be dehumanizing, a word that can be interpreted in many different ways. But these particular criticisms of competitive situations are usually associated with the experience of humiliation. An example of humiliation is when students are embarrassed by the teacher before the rest of the class because they don't know the correct answer or are told publicly they will "never amount to anything" because of their attitude, intellect, or behavior.

Hidden issues and surrogate problems

So, competition has been accused of many detrimental side effects. For example, people claim it incites cheating and other dishonest activities, creates stress, stimulates rivalry, causes shame in defeat, and is a source of envy, despair, selfishness, and callousness (Rich and DeVitis, 1992). It would be easy to accept this argument because it seems intuitive, but with further reflection, we could also point a finger of blame elsewhere, specifically on the individual. Competition can incite bad behavior, but it doesn't have to. There may be an overemphasis on the reward. Still, even blaming the appeal of the reward seems a little unfair, like blaming Helen for Paris's bad behavior. Competition certainly can incite cheating, but it doesn't have to. That depends on the person. At times, competition has been taken so far that competitors seek to win at all costs by injuring or destroying their opponents. This is not necessarily the fault of "competition"; some of the hidden or surrogate problems could be associated with inadequate enforcement of rules by officials, improper socialization, overemphasis on gaining the reward, etc.

To take that thought one step further, it can be especially harmful when the rules that govern the "game" are unfair or unjust. For example, when rules arbitrarily exclude people from benefits, or when people are treated unequally on grounds of race, gender, ethnicity, or religion, citizens complain of discrimination. The quest for equality in education, from the *Brown versus Board of*

Education decision (where separate but equal was determined to be unconstitutional) through affirmative action, has been a priority in the last half of the century. People complain most about competition when they believe that others get ahead, not because they are the most capable or competent, but because of political manipulation, discrimination, or favoritism. This leads people associated with certain groups to denounce competition as a mechanism in our society that categorizes people unfairly. Proponents of competition would argue that most people don't mind healthy competition; what they don't like is when people get ahead (or win) for unjust reasons.

II Work out similarities and differences

Set out central values and outcomes

Competition frequently places the child in a position of seeking to accomplish goals and rewards at the expense of other children. In cooperative activities, goals are linked in a way that one person's aims can only be accomplished through the goal achievements of other group members. Cooperative learners usually try to develop products that are rewarding to all participants. Those that argue competition is harmful and that collaboration is beneficial believe people don't have equal opportunity to compete for rewards. Competition, they say, sorts children unfairly.

Similarities

The competitive approach and the cooperative approach are very different, but they certainly have something in common. Whether children are interacting in cooperative groups or are competing against one another, they are usually more engaged in the activity. The question of whether a teacher should use collaborative or competitive strategies is posed most often in the primary school context (e.g., Mills, 1996). The reason for this is that many people believe that elementary school should be fun. Elementary teachers are often interested in finding ways to capture and hold the limited attention span of young children. Most parents don't want their children turned off by school in the early grades. So, teachers seek strategies that children enjoy in an attempt to give them a positive initial experience in school.

If we move along into high school, we find that teachers may not be as concerned in making learning fun, but most want to prepare students for the real world. In the real world people must compete and they must cooperate. Advocates of both methods would claim they "prepare" children for the real world of work. People must compete, cooperate, and at times learn on their own when they are adults. By having children engage in all of these various activities, not only does a teacher make the pedagogy more interesting, s/he is preparing children for the real world.

It is also interesting to note that competition and cooperation are meant to add enjoyment to the learning process, but these approaches often cause conflict. This could be connected to Piaget's (1954) and Vygotsky's (1986) theories that cognitive dissonance causes conflict, which in turn makes people think and grow. The problem is that unhealthy collaboration can cause conflict that is counterproductive, and a competitive structure in traditional classrooms can sour students by presenting as their only option to be winners or losers. Both strategies have potential dangers associated with generating conflict.

In sum both sides:

- want to find ways to motivate children to learn;
- want children to enjoy learning;
- want to expose children to the real world where competition and collaboration both exist;
- recognize strategies could cause conflict; and
- recognize that competition and cooperation describe a type of interaction with people.

Differences

Competition and cooperation are not exact opposites. If we do not compete, that does not mean we cooperate, and if we do not cooperate, that does mean we compete. Simply stated, competition and cooperation describe interactions with people that are very different. In one extreme, we work with people; in the other, we work against people. Whether a person is competing or cooperating, s/he is using others to somehow propel her/himself forward in her/his goal. When we compete, we compare ourselves to others, which motivates us to do better. When people cooperate, they work together to improve the product.

Competition and cooperation are also different in that they offer different rewards and they evoke different emotional responses. Whether or not we compete or cooperate, the rewards are different. When a person competes, the goal is to win a prize at the expense of others. When people cooperate, they are rewarded by the fact that they enjoy each other's company and they expect to produce a better product or performance by seeking input.

Competition also evokes a different type of emotional response from people. That is not to say that cooperation makes people happy and competition makes people angry. There are those who enjoy competing. When competing, people can feel jealous or angry or excited or proud. When cooperating, people can feel happy or satisfied or frustrated or annoyed. In either case, feelings can be positive or negative, but certainly the emotional responses are different. In sum the differences mentioned are:

- interactions with people are different – with one we are working against people, in the other we are working with people;
- competition and cooperation elicit different emotional responses;
- competition and cooperation set up different reward structures; and

- competition is said to provide opportunities for exclusion and inequity because it is a mechanism in our society that sorts children. Collaboration provides structures for inclusion.

III Rank similarities in order of importance

Isolate the differences in which few have an investment and set them aside

Although this is not a part of the formal procedure, we have ranked the differences in order of importance because we thought it would help us set aside those that are not useful:

1   Competition is said to provide opportunities for exclusion and inequity. Competition is a mechanism in our society that sorts children. Collaboration provides structures for inclusion.
2   Competition and cooperation establish different reward structures.
3   Interactions with people are different: with one we are working against people, in the other we are working with people.
4   They elicit different emotional responses.

In numbers 3 and 4, we find that competition and collaboration present opportunities for people to interact differently and they elicit different emotional responses. This seems unimportant. Usually we don't try to avoid interacting with people or responding emotionally. The last difference can be set aside. Numbers 2 and 3 are truisms. The first is the most significant difference noted.

Rank the similarities in order of importance

In the following list, we have tried to rank the similarities and differences in order of importance.

1   Teachers want to find ways to motivate children to learn.
2   Teachers want children to enjoy learning.
3   Teachers want to expose children to the real world where competition and collaboration both exist.
4   Competition and collaboration often both cause conflict.
5   Both describe a type of interaction with people.

After ranking the similarities and differences, it was interesting that the top-ranked difference was associated with exclusion and inequity. The highest ranked similarity was about motivating children. Perhaps our shared question will be: How do we motivate children in a way that provides opportunities for equitable inclusion?

IV Establish inter-relationships

Define mutual interdependencies

Earlier in the book, we talked about how, in team sport, people must cooperate in order to compete successfully. We provided an example of watching the Super Bowl as a paradigm of competition. To have a cooperative component embedded in a competitive activity is common, not only in sports, but also in classrooms where teachers set up cooperative groups who then compete for rewards. Winning often depends, as in the Super Bowl, on how well people can collaborate.

Beyond this particular inter-relation, however, lie other dependencies. For example, it has been argued that the tension between competition and collaboration produces a balance, not only in education, but also in our society. Competition promotes full use of one's abilities, dispels apathy and stagnation, leads to improved practices, promotes progress, and stimulates advancements in science and other fields (see Rich and DeVitis, 1992). This reminds us of one of the original *Star Trek* episodes where the lead character (the captain of the space ship) was split into two men: one was left with the passive parts of his personality intact, the other was left with his more aggressive traits. Although the two halves were in bitter conflict throughout the show, at the end, the more rational half realizes he needs to regain his aggressive side to be whole again. The moral of the story was that people need their bad side as well as the good. In this show, emotions like anger, jealousy, fear, and suspicion were linked to more positive personal qualities like ambition, hard work, and caution. More or less this is how people are defending competition. Our competitive nature can be useful; perhaps we should find ways to use it productively, rather than denying it or rejecting it.

Another way these two oppositions are inter-related is that at times competition is a direct threat to cooperation. In other words, in many situations, if we set up a competition, children (as well as adults) will not only refrain from helping others, but in some situations sabotage other people's work or efforts. The Johnson brothers (1994) claim that cooperation, which they refer to as "interdependence," results in promotive interaction as individuals encourage each other's efforts to learn. They refer to competition as "negative interdependence" and believe it typically results in oppositional interaction as individuals discourage and obstruct each other's efforts to achieve.

Establish common educational practices

Although many loyal proponents of collaboration sing the praises of cooperative learning, there are practical concerns associated with its implementation. For example, some children become distracted, frustrated, or bored when participating in group activities. And there are many pupils who do not contribute equally to the group's tasks, functions, and goals. How cooperative learning is used in practice determines what it accomplishes. In some cases, children are thrown together with little instruction and guidance and asked to figure things out on their own. Some are monitored and some are not. What happens if children experience conflict? Critics of cooperative learning do not argue against the cooperative ideal, instead they point to problems (the realities) associated with how cooperative learning is implemented.

On the other hand, many teachers do have well-designed cooperative strategies that are impressively implemented in their classrooms. In fact, it seems likely that one reason progressive educators have spent so much time studying and advocating cooperative learning is because it is one progressive strategy that has been successful, and beyond that, actually practical. If teachers choose not to use cooperative strategies, it is probably because they are uncomfortable with the fact that these activities occasionally evoke a type of chaos in the room. During this time, it can be difficult to "control" behavior and "monitor" learning.

Moreover, most educational activities are not organized so that some children win and others lose. For example, although students take tests, and people experience tests as competitive, in most testing situations, tests are not norm referenced. They are criterion referenced. That means that most tests are not graded in comparison to each other (some do well, some do bad, and some fall in between). In criterion-referenced tests, it is possible for all the children taking an exam to answer all the questions correctly. Most teachers do not score children on a curve. Following a strict curve, 33 percent would be scored at the top, the middle, and the bottom. If children were graded on a curve, many more children would actually fail to move ahead.

What is interesting in this situation is that even when people really are not competing for grades, competition is so ingrained in our education system and in our psyche (Tannen, 1998, Chapter 9) that we compete anyway. We may want to foster collaboration, but here, we may need a reality check. Students compete to get 96 points instead of 95 points, even if 95 or better will earn an A grade. In most situations, people still want to do better than others, so they compete when competition need not exist.

Another dramatic example of a situation that is supposed to be competitive but is not, is illustrated in some Special Olympics competitions for young children. In some of these programs, special needs children are set up to compete, yet the Special Olympics staff stress cooperation and fair play over winning. The instructors work to make everyone feel good about their participation. What is interesting is that the activity seems to be set up so that children can experience the joy of competition, but not the pain. Sports for young children without disabilities are supposed to be approached in the same way. The children are there to learn and have fun. This doesn't always happen in reality, especially when parents get competitive as a result of involvement in their child's sports, but the underpinning philosophy of these programs is that children are supposed to enjoy competing and experiencing triumph, while being sheltered from the pain of losing.

Frankly, competition has been considered harmful. Cooperation has been touted as the remedy to many educational ills. Still in practice competition is used extensively in schools to motivate children and cooperative learning is used infrequently (Johnson and Johnson, 1994).

V Formulate the shared problem

Define the problem

At this point, we need to agree upon a shared problem. Some questions that could form the basis for a shared problem include:

- Should children be intrinsically or extrinsically motivated to learn? What is the best way to motivate children to learn?
- Should children be sorted according to ability?
- How do we motivate children in a way that provides opportunities for equitable inclusion?
- What type of people do we want our children to become? Competitive? Cooperative?
- What should children learn? Should teachers focus on teaching skills associated with content or social learning?
- Should all children want (or be expected to collaborate or compete) equally? When should we take into consideration each child's individual personality and interest?

Develop a plan of action

At this point, we have redefined our problem to include the choices listed above. The advocates need to define (choose) a shared problem and begin the discourse procedure over once again. They need to continue the conversation in an attempt to solve their specific concerns. But, since collaboration and competition are not mutually exclusive, it seems quite clear that these approaches should not be structured as an either–or question. A more appropriate question might be: *To what extent do we want children to collaborate and to what extent do we want children to compete?* This question helps us to think about not only how we should teach children, but more importantly, what type of adults we want our children to become.

Reflection and speculation

By now, you may be noticing a pattern. Once again some of our shared questions are associated with what should children learn. Should children be sorted according to ability? How do we motivate children? It is interesting that with the math opposition, and now with competition and collaboration, many of the questions that lay the foundation for these oppositions are similar, if not the same. This would suggest that if we came to some agreement or at least authentic acceptance of our stances on the old debates in education, we might move forward in our goal to stop the pendulum. We would never stop the conversation, but we might have faster forward progress. If we can't agree on the goal, we can't agree on the approach. Also, with competition and collaboration, what struck us as important was this was a difficult opposition to compare because it had inter-relations. Teachers often set up competition between collaborative groups. Therefore competition is often embedded in collaborative environments.

Would it be possible to eliminate competition and/or collaboration completely? That solution seems unrealistic. In speculation, what does our analysis suggest so far? It can easily be argued that cooperative learning is useful and should be used as a classroom strategy much more extensively, especially since it is seldom used. At the time of their research, the Johnson brothers found that class activities were structured cooperatively only for 7 to 20 percent of the time (Johnson and Johnson, 1989). We are told that cooperative learning should be used whenever teachers want students to learn more, like school better, like each other better, have higher self-esteem, and learn more effective social skills. Competitive strategies are used when teachers want students to earn better scores on standardized tests or to memorize material for other reasons. All are used in an effort to engage children in learning activities. It seems possible that advocates might decide that teachers should use cooperative strategies as much as possible, use competition less often, while being careful to address the serious concerns that people have about competition. Perhaps building on the best would suggest allowing more activities where children compete in cooperative situations. Certainly, that would simulate a real-world adult work-based team trying to develop the newest piece of software or design a new building. It is possible that people would decide to use both strategies and carefully consider and attend to the concerns of both. Ultimately, defining the problem and developing solutions will depend on the context and it will depend on whether people are dedicated to finding a solution that builds on the best.

Now that we have worked through a couple of controversies, including the math education and competition and collaboration, in the next chapter we elaborate the conditions and the requirements for participation in RD.

5 The conditions and requirements for RD

In the controversies that we have discussed, we have noted the possibility, even the likelihood, that some people embroiled in the controversies will not be interested in reconciliation or a discourse which embodies it. It makes sense to us to say that the core of RD is moral and intellectual, and that it is rooted in a new vision of civil discussion. If that is correct, then the specific conditions and requirements for participation will have to be hugely different from those for participants in antagonistic debate. These are not just formal conditions: they imply habits of mind, moral and intellectual dispositions, perhaps even changed character and temperament. We need to explore these possibilities.

The conditions for participation

As we talked to people about our idea of reconciliation, various kinds of entrenched ideas were mentioned. Some teachers think minority children are inferior. Some psychologists think that genetics is the only determinant of ability. Some people believe that wealthy children should have better access to education, others that women should not be educated much, if at all. Citing these kinds of views, people consistently asked two questions:

- "Aren't there some oppositions that cannot be reconciled?"
- "Aren't there some oppositions that should not be reconciled?"

The answer to the first question is a pragmatic one. First, there may be people who refuse to reconcile their position, those who simply state what it is and turn their backs. Second, there may well be positions where people have the will to reconcile, but cannot find common ground.

The answer to the second question is more important because it centers on people's moral beliefs. We came up against this problem specifically in our writing of the chapter on testing (see Chapter 7). Some critics of testing go so far as to say that testing damages children and is therefore immoral. We assume this is a minority belief, given that educators do a lot of testing. Still, many of us have had unfortunate personal experiences with testing, or are resentful and angry at test results because we have been locked out of opportunities as a consequence. It poses the question whether believers in the fundamental immorality of testing could engage in RD on the topic. These ruminations moved us to the general question: Are there beliefs that would rule out a person from RD altogether? We provisionally saw three categories, which might make RD impossible. We posed three questions:

- Is the position held by this person rooted in an unshakeable moral belief? For example, it would be difficult to hold authentic RD on the biology curriculum if one participant were a doctrinaire believer in creationism (see Chapter 8).
- Is the position held by this person a challenge to constitutionally enshrined practice? For example, it would be difficult to hold RD about a school curriculum if one participant believes that there should be universal education for whites only.
- Is the position held by this person a breach of existing law? For example, it would be difficult to hold RD if, in discussing sex education, a participant believes that the laws against incest can be ignored or should be repealed.

But then we sought to put the three questions in positive form as conditions for taking part. Two considerations were in our mind as we did this. First, we don't want RD always to drift back to a discussion of first principles of law and morality. Some base has to be articulated on which people can start, recognizing of course that no single law, even the tenets of the Constitution, is forever fixed and unchanging. But, second, there are educational and teaching conventions resting on a moral base (such as teachers' avoidance of sarcasm or teasing). Again, while there is room for discussion about such matters, RD is not intended as theoretical, but as practical. There must be some givens for such a discussion. Thus, we concluded, participants in RD must be:

- open to moral and ideological reconciliation;
- committed to the Constitution which can set parameters for discussion; and
- believe that people, in principle, ought to obey the law.

If these conditions are not met, we believe that the discussion is going to be difficult to start and, if it does, it will probably founder, even if the participants come to the table believing they are intellectually and morally committed to the process. There can come a time, in other words, when advocates should give up the reconciliatory process and move on. Otherwise it is a waste of time. For RD is not some kind of panacea or magic wand out of which consensus will emerge among diametrically opposed views, or among participants whose convictions are beyond certainty. RD is a gritty, unending, moral and intellectual struggle.

But take care! These conditions might beguile us into refraining from entering potentially valuable RD. Don't give up too quickly or stereotype people according to faulty assumptions. Don't assume that people can't meet these conditions before talking to them. Just because people do not share the same religious beliefs does not mean they do not share some similar moral values. Beyond the labels "atheist" and "Christian" there may be deeply held and common views of the child upon which an agreed practice can evolve out of RD. People may believe there is a huge gulf in their views of learning, but may be surprised by the level of agreement. A person may think another person has a totally different view of the family, yet her/his view of family roles and responsibilities may be much like her/his own. These are matters for exploration through discourse, not for prejudiced (before the fact) decision.

The requirements for participants in RD

Let us suppose then that all participants meet the conditions. What then are the basic requirements for effective participation? They fall into two categories:

- attitudes, beliefs, and competencies; and
- disciplines of the discourse.

These requirements are not prior conditions. People dedicated to RD don't have to have them before they start, they can learn them as they go along. Indeed we regard RD as a potentially most effective vehicle for learning, and we expect people will want to develop or refine these personal qualities through experience of RD. Each category of requirements can be continuously redefined and improved.

Participants' attitudes, beliefs, and competencies

Respect for where people are coming from

In our development of these arguments, we found early on that it is always necessary to understand the background to the diverse views people hold. Obviously people are influenced by their own upbringing, especially, as we noted in the introductory chapter, where educational matters are discussed. All of us are heirs to different kinds of traditions and we need to locate them in RD, for they are reflected in the choices made in specific contexts. We have various types of commitments and choices in mind.

First, there are personal involvements. Is a person an advocate of standardized tests because s/he performs well at them or an opponent because they upset her/his children? Is a person opposed to school choice because s/he lives in a "good" neighborhood? Is a person a proponent of school choice because s/he no longer has children in school and wouldn't have to deal with the consequences? This can be expanded into personal background and autobiography, good and bad experiences. Then there are contextual choices people make, for example decisions to pay more attention to one's career than to one's children's education. Finally, there are choices rooted in basic beliefs or *ideology* and, of course, those not rooted in any particular ideology at all. A person with a free-market view of the economy may take the same view of public education, perhaps without examining the differences. A religious teacher may need a job while at the same time feel upset at being unable to express her/his religious commitments.

The process of RD, because it is couched in moral terms, demands that the position of contributors, and the choices they make, be understood. We need both the history of the (theoretical) oppositions and the story of how individual participants came to hold the views they do.

Accept responsibility for the fairness of a discussion

All children are morally worthy of our respect. Public educational policy constantly faces the problem of being fair to all children and just in the distribution of resources. Here are three examples of problems created by the principle of fairness. First, many of us recall the public discussion when HIV was first identified about children who were born with AIDS, or children with family members who had AIDS. Neighborhood parents panicked because they had no detailed information, inflicting additional burdens of public shame on these children who were not to blame. Recall, second, the widespread discussions about mainstreaming children with differing degrees of mental and physical handicap, and also how the language of "being challenged" seeks to supplant the implicit inequity contained in that notion of handicap. Third, debates about school re-districting often contain high-flown phrases which, when cut down to their essence, mean "we don't want our children mixing with that riff-raff." These are, publicly speaking, three relatively contentious areas for discussion each of which is rooted in the principles of fairness and distributive justice.

Without prejudging any of these three cases, critical to RD is the idea of fairness. Authorities, especially, need to consider how to be fair. Too often, public debate is conducted about "them," those people who have neither the skills nor the confidence to enter a public forum even as a listener. Some discussions simply don't accommodate those who don't speak English well. Some people can be excluded because they are thought not to be educated, even though the discussion might concern their children. Fairness demands opportunity. Most parents care desperately about their children, but may be very ill equipped to enter public discussion that affects them as citizens and parents. Central to the idea of public debate, but critical to RD, must be that we anticipate and value additional information and opportunities to contribute from anyone.

Understand and recognize the subtleties in the use of language

Language obviously can be used in all kinds of ways, and persuasion and rhetoric are part of any discourse. Yet we also have to constantly watch the way language is used, especially in terms of its persuasive power. Ruth Mitchell provides us with an excellent example of persuasive writing, which, on the face of it, doesn't seem promising for reconciliation:

Evaluation sends a message. It points to what is valued and ignores what is not perceived to be important. Educational evaluation – testing and assessment – has been *telling* students, teachers and administrators, and legislators that the *system values rote memorization and passive recognition of single correct answers.* This message has been powerfully conveyed by the ubiquitous multiple-choice tests which have *dominated* American educational evaluation for most of the past thirty years and have *terrorized* it in the 1980's.

(Mitchell, 1992; our emphasis)

Many of the words selected here are adjectives, adverbs, or strong verbs. Look carefully. The word "telling" is putting students, teachers, legislators, and administrators in a passive (and unpleasant) role where someone is telling them what to do. With the next word, Mitchell demonizes the system (which is not hard because we all hate "the system" right?). And finally the words "dominated" and "terrorized" are certainly very strong! If we rewrite the text it says the same thing and yet conveys a different, non-pejorative message:

Educational evaluation – testing and assessment – has been communicating to students, teachers and administrators and legislators that people value memorization and recognition of individual correct answers. This message has been presented by the multiple-choice tests which have been associated with American educational evaluation for most of the past thirty years, especially prevalent in the 1980's.

Of course, Ruth Mitchell is trying to persuade the reader, with sound arguments, to use other forms of assessment besides testing. She believes testing is detrimental. The quoted paragraph and her many comments throughout the book demonstrate that she is not only concerned with testing, but also concerned with societal values that have broader implications, a perspective with which we are sympathetic. One of her goals is to convince people who do not share her values to reconsider their position. She is trying to move society (that means us!) closer to consensus with regard to what we value. She realizes this is at the heart of the controversy. Her writing is powerful and, with it, she effectively makes progress in her goal. In this book, we had a similar goal for the introductory chapter. Our writing in that chapter was meant to be more persuasive. We were seeking an emotional response, as well as an intellectual response.

Search consistently for the similarities in the positions under discussion

Accustomed as we are to confrontation, we can be led to think that differences are more likely than similarities. We should be much more circumspect about profound divisions for perhaps there is much greater agreement about education than one might suspect.

Disciplines of the discourse

We were both amazed by how quickly Jack and Garrett learned to grasp language in dialogue. With children, statements and other questions quickly replace the insistent and repetitive "what's that?" They get the complexity of language exchanges quickly, something they can only learn by doing. Hence the importance of talking to young children almost unceasingly, tiring though that may be. You can only learn RD by doing it, too.

Yet it is a common experience, we are sure, to be in a conversation with a person who thinks s/he is participating, but is in fact doing things that undermine the discussion. For example, there are those who rehearse platitudes (we all care about each other here, don't we?), which takes a serious conversation nowhere. We have heard others completely ignore a theme going on in a discussion and make remarks which are completely irrelevant (I forgot to mention that we should consider X). Others still can interject by demanding the right to be heard as a representative of some group or other (as a member of Y, I can tell you …). But perhaps the most common weakness to which we are all subject is that of stereotyping individuals. In education we can hear phrases like: "You testing people, you all believe human beings are just like machines!" "You progressives, you believe we should never discipline children!" "You advocates of school choice, you believe in a free for all in which the rich will win!" Or, of course, more polite versions.

From his school-teaching days, Hugh remembers a colleague had a fascinating response from a boy in his class to *Death of a Salesman*, the play by Arthur Miller. The boy said that a play which has a dialogue where people don't talk when others are talking couldn't represent most family life: for in his experience, everyone always shouted at once! Conversations need discipline. We tried to think of types of discipline specific to a participant in RD, because we believe that many people don't have a conception or experience of a disciplined conversation. Each of these disciplines we mention is built into the RD procedure (Chapter 3) and the protocol (in the Appendix):

- Listening.
- Expressing oneself effectively.
- Careful personal interaction.
- Searching and learning through deliberation.

Of course we are aware that such disciplines will apply in many other contexts than that of reconciling educational aims, but RD gives each a different emphasis. The requirements for such discipline, both of the individual and the group, are outlined here and they are embedded in the protocol.

The discipline of listening

Obviously people have lots to say, as the success of Internet chat rooms and home pages indicate, but do they listen? Failure to listen can of course have many causes, one of which is the false assumption we make about the person talking. A teacher might think parents who don't come to school to talk about their child are uncaring and disinterested. From the parents' viewpoint, they may feel they are never listened to, merely talked at. Election rituals are usually in a question-and-answer format, which is not, of course, a conversation and when it's all over, the private citizen gets quickly out of touch with elected representatives. This person is very much in touch with the agents of government, the public officials in the IRS, HUD (Housing and Urban Development), Social Security, or their equivalents at state and local levels. Whether it is paying your taxes, or building a home or buying one, or taking your children to school, you meet the officials! Their job is to carry out policy, not question its efficacy. It doesn't help to establish a framework of listening if people approach officials with hostility, or other forms of uncivil behavior.

Listening can be very difficult for officials, especially where it is not a policy they have designed or one that, privately, they would not support. Schools are unlikely to seek your input on major policy decisions, though they will be unwise if they fail to go through the motions on matters of political controversy, like re-districting. Indeed officials (elected and appointed) have all kinds of devices for "involving the public." They set up a committee that invites comments. They establish a policy and ask for questions. Often the private citizen ignores these invitations because s/he senses that the decisions have already been made and this is an exercise in window-dressing democracy. But is this really listening, or merely listening to the vocal, or the special interest?

But look at it from the officials' viewpoint for a moment. They believe that they are going to get arguments from fixed special interest positions (which they already know). They believe they will get versions of familiar oppositions. They know the arguments about school choice versus neighborhood schools, about testing and assessment, and all the special interest protagonists will do is to trot out well-worn clichés from these positions. They know too that most people who contribute will want to declare their position forthrightly and will be more interested in winning than in seeking a common solution. Officials know all this – because that is the way things continue to operate.

The discipline of listening is not a skill of one's ear, as if we can flex our hearing as we can our calf muscles. Listening, we believe, is a moral commitment. To listen with sufficient care, we must be interested in what the other person has to say! It demands at least the following:

- not assuming that we know what a person is going to say;
- finding a way (e.g., by writing down) to get at exactly what a person means;
- never making assumptions about where the person is coming from;
- rarely interrupting; and
- asking more questions than making statements.

RD puts a huge premium on the discipline of listening.

The discipline of self-expression

This discipline is also not a skill of the mouth and brain. It is a moral commitment to explain what we think to others who value our right to say it and who value the content of what we have to say. People often become so emotionally invested in a particular position that they cannot think straight. Others are inhibited by conversation, especially in any sort of public forum (remember how silent you were in class?). Some are over-talkative, as if on automatic pilot, unable to halt the flow of words pouring out of their mouths. Some don't think before they talk. Many good public speakers are appalling conversationalists, though that may be because they are not interested in listening. None of this is easy. It all demands practice. If RD is to work, there must be a conscious attention to the discipline of self-expression that is connected to, but different from, listening.

The discipline of self-expression therefore seems to us to demand

- careful practice, based on notes or a written script;
- constant support from all participants;
- a focus on thinking of questions to ask, not statements to make;
- monitoring the styles of other participants; and
- a sense of moral obligation to make oneself clear.

The discipline of personal interaction

The most central requirement of RD is that participants must want mutual success. Making the comparison with a team in any game can easily convey this. Anyone who has been a member of a team knows that team success is more important than individual success, though all the time there will be tensions between players on the same side who are in competition with each other for cash, public esteem, or whatever. RD is like a team activity, *except* that members have different positions to start with, and are thus openly in some kind of competitive stance. It is through personal interaction that mutual success is obtained and through which the competitive stance can be dissipated.

These may be called skills of personal interaction, provided they are recognized as being moral not technical. They include such propensities as:

- resisting any temptation to stereotype or deliberately misinterpret another person;
- paying particular attention to those who find difficulty in taking part in the discussion (see Belenky *et al.*, 1986);
- deliberately engaging personally with every participant; and
- accepting mutual responsibility for the conduct of the discussion.

The discipline of searching and learning through deliberation

People are often blinded by their prejudices, but to take part in RD is to be prepared to search for understanding, critical to mutual success. The discipline requires that everyone comes to the table as a learner, not a knower. It goes further than that, however: for it is to understand that everyone else has something to teach us, whether they be young or old, rich or poor, or wherever they are coming from. This searching and learning is not a book study. It occurs within the process of deliberation, which demands valuing democratic procedures set within the purpose of the deliberation, in this case the reconciliation of educational aims. So participants must also *learn* these disciplines of discourse.

Habits of mind and dispositions

So far we have isolated basic moral notions, like respect and responsibility for fairness, individual talents which are also moral in different ways such as listening, expressing oneself clearly, learning how to interact with others, and we have discussed briefly the ability to search out similarities in opposed positions.

Yet there are habits of mind and dispositions that are integrative of these various qualities but also extend into both intellectual quality and emotional dispositions. The procedure we described in Chapter 3 can be viewed as a set of habits of mind that provide a structure for defining problems. For example, in the RD procedure, a person has to first locate what the issues are under discussion. In this step, we seek to understand the context of the debate. That requires patience and perseverance, as well as a critical habit of mind that is controlled by the concern to understand positions one does not hold. We are not saying, by using such "virtue" terms, that RD is reserved only for those of saintly disposition. Rather, we know that our aggressive skills and dispositions can be sharpened constantly if we engage in antagonistic debate. Equally, our reconciliatory dispositions have been neglected and left fallow. Habits of mind and dispositions are learned: they are not given to us at birth.

In the next step, we recommended a search for similarities. Searching for similarities will also require patience and perseverance, but it will also demand the ability to suspend rather than rush to judgment, to hold back one's emotional charges or prejudices, and to ponder, to ruminate, to consider almost in a judicial way the possibilities of linkages between what appear to be dramatically different positions. Nowhere is this matter more clearly expressed than in Deborah Tannen's (1993) book *You Just Don't Understand*, which challenges men and women to understand those dissimilarities and to work to understand and maybe to adopt the dispositional frameworks of the other gender.

Yet we are also going to have to deliberate between important and unimportant similarities and differences. In the third step in our procedure, we asked people to rank the similarities, focus on those that are important, and disregard those that are not. The habits of mind appropriate to deliberation are not necessarily the strengths of people who prefer quick action. This habit goes beyond mere rumination and pondering. It demands a disposition to accept changes in beliefs and habits of mind such as consistency in examining all positions. It also demands a certain kind of rigor to which one is passionately committed. For it has often been argued that reason is cold and calculating, whereas passion is free, warm, and uninhibited. Our belief is that we need to be passionate about reason, and to move away from those antagonistic habits of mind, which undermine our reason and reasoned dialogue. For this, judgment is extremely important. Nowhere will these habits be of more value than in trying to rank similarities and differences between positions.

In the next step of the procedure, we considered the inter-relations. We will also need the clarity of mind to be explicit about our values. This is both very easy and very difficult. For example, a person who believes in a position derived, say, from a theological argument has simply to deploy the theological position and defend it from a fixed premise. That, we think, is relatively easy. It is much more difficult for a person whose disposition is inquisitive, who is reluctant to accept authority, for s/he can see all manner of difficulty in her/his own position which makes its articulation very problematic. At this stage, it is important to be honest about the realities of the situation and to avoid the trap of polarizing oppositions in an attempt to defend one's position.

Notice that we have set out a complex set of habits and dispositions. That does not mean, we repeat, that we cannot enter RD unless we have them. Rather, that we need to adopt these varied attitudes, disciplines, and dispositions if RD is to be fruitful for us. For many of us, we are old (and young) dogs needing to learn new tricks.

Summary

We have set out three conditions for participants in RD: that they are open to moral and ideological reconciliation, committed to constitutional and legal parameters as a basis for discussion, and not advocates of breaking the law.

We have also established requirements for participants which are the disciplines of the discourse, namely listening, expressing oneself effectively, personal interaction, and searching and learning through deliberation.

We have finally sketched some habits of mind and dispositions that we believe are fruitful to contemplate. All will take a more detailed shape in the protocol (see the Appendix), which will also set out recommendations for chairing the discussion and keeping a record.

We now look at the school choice controversy.

6 Where should children go to school?

The school choice controversy

The choice controversy provides a perfect topic for reconciliation and for further refining the conditions and requirements for RD because, as Eric Boyer stated, "There's an intensity, even zealousness in the debate on school choice that smothers thoughtful discourse" (Carnegie Foundation for the Advancement of Teaching, 1992). In the absence of convincing evidence for either side, the choice controversy continues to cause disagreement among scholars that is amplified through the popular press. In our own personal experience, both of us were exposed to different aspects of school choice. Hugh's father, who was an Anglican (Episcopalian) clergyman, sent his children through a private prep school and then to boarding school and then on to Oxford. Although the family had few resources, his father was determined to send his children to the "right schools." As a young child, Pamela attended neighborhood public schools, but in high school, she was free to choose any school in her district. Even then, in the late 1970s/early 1980s, her home state had mandated a form of school choice. Was this useful for her? Since her family moved quite a bit while she was in high school, if she had been forced to go to neighborhood schools, she would have attended approximately four–five high schools by the end of her school career. As it was, she only attended two high schools.

Embedded in the details of our own educational experiences are questions common to the "school choice" controversy. Should the public help pay for private education? Do parents have the ability to choose good schools? Should the government pay for transportation? Can the free market improve educational quality? These are questions that were then, and are still, part of the ongoing debate.

I Locate the issues

Describe the oppositions and their origins

School choice is not easily described. It comes in many flavors. Choice can be limited to public schools or it can include private schools. Choice options can include voluntary or involuntary open enrollment policies or magnet schools. Five options are described below (from Young and Clinchy, 1992):

(a) Alternative and magnet schools serve at-risk students. They are usually organized around themes or specialized programs such as literacy, math/science or the arts.
(b) Second chance options allow unsuccessful students to attend public schools outside of their district. In some cases children can attend private educational clinics or learning centers at state expense.
(c) Postsecondary options allow high school juniors and seniors to enroll in colleges and receive both high school and college credit.
(d) Inter-district choice plans allow students to choose from among any of the school districts within a state.
(e) Intra-district choice allows children to enroll anywhere within a district.

Another alternative is the charter school option. According to Yancey (2000), charter schools are deregulated public schools that can be created by a group of parents, teachers, community educators, or entrepreneurs with approval from a state or local sponsor. They can be reconstituted from existing public or private schools, or they can be newly created. In his book on choice, Sarason (1998) states:

> the charter school movement is the most radical challenge ever to the existing system. Although it has never been stated, let alone recognized, by national and state political leadership, you do not have to be a logician to conclude that charter schools are based on the opinion that the present system is by itself incapable of reforming itself.
>
> (p. 52)

This reform has gained momentum in the last few years. Yancey (2000) claims that only 100 charter schools were in operation just three years after the first school opened in Minnesota in 1992. By 2001, over 250,000 students are enrolled in over 1,700 charter schools across the country. Finally, there is also a *de facto* choice within the public sector among the better-off, for they can choose houses within school catchment areas, a fact that has not gone unnoticed by realtors. But this is not a formal choice system.

   We are told that the choice controversy became visible in the 1960s and 1970s when a few liberals started advocating vouchers as a way to achieve greater equity for disadvantaged children (see Hanus and Cookson, 1996; Cibulka, 1990). Choice has a complicated political history. According to Morken and Formicola (1999):

> There are many demands on the public sector to balance the prerogatives of parents and students with regard to education, with the perceived obligation of the government to provide schooling for America's children. As a

result, there is constant, yet subtle, dynamic interplay between politics, the law, and interest groups; an internal tension simultaneously militates against, and makes possible, school choice in the United States now and in the future.

(p. 15)

It has never enjoyed broad support across ideological differences and partisan group interests in the public sector. Why? Past reform efforts under the umbrella of choice have been viewed as disjointed with no unifying theme (Cibulka, 1990). Vouchers and tax credits raise controversies that have surrounded aid to private schools such as whether this aid is constitutional given our dedication to the separation of church and state. Magnet and other specialty schools initially were associated with racial desegregation. Today, these schools have generated new controversies about "creaming" that draw criticism for a new type of segregation (Cibulka, 1990). At the heart of the choice issue is the idea of trusting people to make "good" decisions. The struggle between telling someone where their child has to go to school and letting everyone choose is at the poles of a collectivist or a libertarian view.

Hidden issues and surrogate problems

Some possible hidden issues and surrogate problems associated with the choice controversy were referred to earlier in the book. Does the superintendent want more control of the schools in her/his district? Do parents want more power to censor the books their children are required to read? Since the choice/neighborhood school controversy is a policy issue it has its foundations in the question "who has power?" The hidden issues and surrogate problem possibilities have to be faced because of the dilemma of choice as a policy confronts individuals who must take a stance based on their own interests or on what might be termed the common good.

II Work out similarities and differences

Set out central values and outcomes

The controversy surrounding school choice differs markedly from the other controversies we have tried to reconcile because we have taken the controversy out of the classroom for the purpose of exploring a policy issue. The choice controversy has been linked to private school aid, which was objectionable to the political left. Then it was tied to desegregation, which was resisted by the political right. Since then, however, these distinctions have been blurred and now this reform is usually associated with public schools. Choice is now a policy issue considered by some to be an egalitarian belief in the local control of schools. The left is still wary because although this reform has its origins in a liberal attempt to produce a more equitable system for disadvantaged children, the left worries it will do just the opposite. It worries that the schools will become more stratified as a result of faulty choice implementation. People on the political right are still wary because although they believe that the free market can motivate quality, in practice the choice option is more expensive than traditional public education. So, within this controversy we have overlapping political agendas that can become quite complex, especially for those trying to make a decision for one position or another.

Similarities

By analyzing the choice conflict, we were able to demonstrate how both groups share many underlying goals within this oppositional frame. As we considered the similarities, we found advocates on both sides who:

- agree that education needs to be improved. Nobody on either side is willing to say that schools don't need improvement. Some argue that the schools are in decline, but even those people would admit that schools have improved in some ways over the last 30 years. Those who believe that the schools are not in decline would never be so bold as to suggest that schools are perfect. In the literature, most admit right away that schools are facing serious problems today, especially in large downtown urban areas. Both groups admit that schools need to be improved; the question is how much change do they need, and what is the best strategy for change?;
- have as a goal to help disadvantaged children have better access to education. Both groups agree that children from poor backgrounds need better access to education. Both agree that children from privileged backgrounds have better access to education and therefore have better opportunities to succeed in life;
- want to ensure equity, eliminate racial segregation and class stratification without court-ordered busing. Both groups are interested in ameliorating racial segregation and class stratification. In fact, the impetus for these changes was inspired by the desire to integrate children, but in a way that avoids court-ordered busing;
- agree that good schools are difficult to implement (public schools or choice schools). What that means is that it is very hard to design and implement programs that accomplish certain goals (e.g., racial integration). Both are considered expensive.

Differences

We found the most significant differences between both sides, and which we need to elaborate on, were:

- Whether or not and how much schools are in decline.

- How we can improve educational opportunity for disadvantaged children including how to ameliorate race and class segregation.
- How the schools should be governed (local versus central office control).
- How we can motivate schools to improve. Through free-market or societal obligation? Are private schools better?
- Whether or not (and how) parents can make appropriate choices.

Are schools in decline?

The tension between advocates and opponents of choice is embedded in the question of whether Americans should provide common educational experiences necessary for a common foundation of shared knowledge and values, or whether we should allow American parents to find ways to educate their children as they see fit. As evidence to support their positions, both sides point to conflicting views regarding the decline of American education. Those who want choice believe the educational system is failing and needs to undergo a major change. Those who oppose choice claim that the decline in American education is a myth (Meier and Smith, 1995; Pearson, 1993; Bracey, 1994).

People who believe schools are in decline often point to test score data to support their claims (see Henig, 1994). Those who do not believe schools are in decline try to discredit statistical evidence that supports this view (see Meier and Smith, 1995; Pearson, 1993; Bracey, 1994). For example, those who believe in the decline point to the drop in SAT scores as evidence to support their beliefs. Those who resist this view believe that the primary reason for SAT declines is not the diminishing quality of education, but the changes in demographics. They argue that in the 1970s most of the students taking the SAT ranked in the top 20 percent of their high school class. Today, an increasing number of test takers must learn English as a second language and many are now minorities and women, who tend to score lower on achievement tests. Those who believe the schools are not in decline further point to the fact that while minorities have tended to score lower on the tests, all minority groups have improved their SAT scores in the past 15 years (Meier and Smith, 1995, p.16). Those who do not believe schools are in decline claim that if the scores were weighted to reflect the demographic makeup of the 1975 pool of test takers, that would show that scores actually improved by 30 points in the last 15 years (Sandia National Laboratories, 1993, pp. 267–270).

What is best for disadvantaged children?

Both groups believe that a primary goal of choice and of public schooling is to provide equitable educational opportunity to disadvantaged children. Choice advocates argue that without choice, parents are left with no alternative if their child is being treated unfairly or is not getting an appropriate or adequate education.

People who argue against choice believe that it can actually hurt disadvantaged children. They believe that when parents pull their children out of neighborhood schools, those who are left are children from families who do not understand how to make choices, do not feel they have options (e.g., due to transportation problems), or do not care where their children go to school. For society to expect an entire population of people in poorer neighborhoods to gravitate toward the suburbs is unrealistic. Transportation and information costs pose barriers to student participation in a school choice system, as do the dictates of building space. People fear the children who benefit from choice will be those who suffer the fewest disadvantages, while those who suffer the most will be made to suffer more.

Perpetuation of race and class segregation

The question about whether choice is helpful for disadvantaged children is tied to the question of whether choice (or lack of choice) perpetuates race and class segregation. Those who argue for choice claim that if children are forced to attend neighborhood schools, and the neighborhoods are segregated (which they often are), then the children have no choice but to be segregated in schools. Those who oppose choice argue that if we allow children to go anywhere they wish and especially if we give children money to go to private schools, the only ones left in public schools will be the least motivated and the least supported.

It has also been suggested that if parents are free to choose schools, some will use this as an excuse to take their children out of schools that are integrated (by class or race) and put them in schools that are segregated. This accusation is most often associated with white middle-class parents, but some ethnic minority parents might also want their children to attend minority schools because they believe that in this environment, their children will develop a better sense of self.

Can the free market improve educational quality?

Choice advocates claim that market economics can cure ailing schools in the United States. Competition will provide incentive to improve test scores, which, from this perspective, constitutes improvement in educational quality.

The critics of school choice argue this promise has never been confirmed (see Sosniak and Ethington, 1992). They point to research studies that state they cannot corroborate the promised benefits of choice (Henig, 1994). The Carnegie Foundation for the Advancement of Teaching (1992) claims that although choice does indeed provide important benefits in specific cases, overall the impact is mixed. Specifically, it found that the academic benefits were mixed, participation in existing programs was low, and choice was extremely expensive to implement and sustain. It also found that when choice was studied in other countries, the results were also mixed or disappointing (see Adler *et al.*, 1989; Bowe *et al.*, 1992).

If we examine the motivation of those who advocate choice, their strong feelings are often rooted in personal experience (or in research) that has convinced them that private school education is better than public school education. Those who believe educational politics should not be defined by market ideology are also passionate about their beliefs. Engel (2000) claims that

> current day discussions about the future of education are conducted almost entirely in the language of the free market: individual achievement, competition, choice, economic growth, and national security – with only occasional lip service being given to egalitarian and democratic goals.
>
> (p. 3)

Those who believe in private schools claim they are safer, smaller, attract more serious students, and produce better results. Is this true? According to the *Washington Times* (1994), 78 percent of non-public school students took college preparatory courses, while only 52 percent of public school students took college preparatory classes. In 1993–1994, private school pupils had an average SAT verbal score of 443 compared to 419 for public school students. In math they earned 480 compared to 477.

Advocates on both sides find ways to defend their positions and discredit statistical evidence, however. In an example of this, a group of choice proponents cited statistical evidence to support the argument that market-driven schools were superior to democratically controlled schools in producing higher achievement scores. The group highlighted a situation where tests were given to a group of sophomores and then again to the same students when they were seniors. Therefore only the change in scores that occurred during high school were used in an effort to eliminate the effects of prior history. This seems like a good research design. But critics argued that just because someone measures gain scores from one year to the next does not mean that backgrounds (and all other influences) cease to operate between the 10th and 12th grades (Hanus and Cookson, 1996).

Who should have power? Local schools? Central office? NEA (National Education Association)?

Why are some people persuaded that private schools are better than public schools? As was mentioned earlier, many believe quality is significantly affected by organizational structure (Chubb and Moe, 1990). Two perspectives are provided on the organization of public schools. One view holds that public schools should be centralized, bureaucratic, and hierarchically subordinate to other administrative agencies and democratic institutions. In contrast to this view, the other holds that schools should be part of a decentralized system, which provides local autonomy and independence among relevant participants. Choice advocates, those who believe schools are unresponsive, see the former and want the latter (Meier and Smith, 1995).

School choice calls for eliminating the governing structures of schools in favor of decentralization and deregulation. Choice advocates argue that control by democratic institutions promotes ineffective organization and limits autonomy, which constrains the schools to respond appropriately to the educational demands of the community (Chubb and Moe, 1990). As one advocate put it, schools are forced to serve their democratic masters, not parents and students. Because education is a monopoly, students do not have the option to seek a better school, and schools have no incentives to change. Choice supporters see private schools as less constrained by politics than public schools, and it is this autonomy that is the key to their success. In the public system, legislatures and school boards set goals and enforce compliance through a bureaucratic hierarchy. Bureaucracies require forms, procedures, and auditing mechanisms. These requirements limit the actions schools may take.

On the other side of the argument, those who oppose choice claim that two decades of research about what contributes to effective schools have resulted in a consensus about the essential qualities of highly productive schools. These qualities are a positive and academically serious school climate, positive discipline and control, an effective and strong principal, staff development, the monitoring of clearly established goals and objectives, autonomy, and parental involvement. None of those qualities are tied to school governance and critics believe there is little, if any, reliable scholarly research that links school governance with student achievement (see Hanus and Cookson, 1996). Moreover, some research suggests that local governance does not cure the problems associated with politics and the special interests of people who are focused on the different aims of education (Yancey, 2000; Sarason, 1998). "Despite the rhetoric that charter schools were going to be hothouses of reform, the results are mixed," says Bruce Fuller, of the University of California, Berkeley. "We have to ask if charters are beset by the same problems as garden-variety public schools" (Morse, 2001).

How do parents choose?

Another argument against choice is associated with parents' ability to make choices for their children. Brighouse (2000, p. 192) points to a number of research studies that conclude that (a) the ability to choose is associated with social class and level of education of the parent, (b) the non-choosers frequently went along with the preference of their children, (c) most of those who did choose had little information on how to make the choice, and (d) among those who did choose, academic concerns were not ranked at the top of their list of concerns. Those who assert that parents don't always make rational choices claim it is normal. They believe human beings don't always make rational choices because we are subject to passion, fear, and violence. They would argue that irrational behavior should not be considered good or bad, simply part of the human condition.

III Rank similarities in order of importance

Isolate the differences in which few have an investment and set them aside

The differences we uncovered in this controversy were serious issues that were well argued on both sides, and they were differences, for the most part, on which agreement was unlikely.

Rank the similarities in order of importance

We chose to rank the similarities according to what the advocates might choose:

1   Have as a goal to help disadvantaged children have better access to education.
2   Want to ensure equity, eliminate racial segregation, and class stratification.
3   Want to avoid court-ordered busing.
4   Agree that education needs to be improved.
5   Agree that good schools are difficult to implement (public or choice schools).
6   Agree that either approach is expensive.

IV Establish inter-relationships

Establish common educational practices

As we sought to better understand the mutual dependencies and practical inter-relations embedded in choice schools versus neighborhood schools, we started thinking more seriously about the role of the parents in the process of school choice. How is choice implemented in practice? How do they learn about choice?

Where choice is an option and there has been an irreconcilable disagreement between the parents and school, neither party is trapped in an undesirable situation. Many a parent, teacher, or principal has no doubt been relieved to have the freedom to simply move a child away from a school and make a fresh start. These situations apart, do parents use choice options, and what are the criteria for choice? Some claim that parents don't use choice options very often even when they are available. It is quite likely that the majority of people are not concerned with the possibility that various schools provide grossly different levels of educational quality. If people truly believed there was a significant difference between schools, they would certainly make better use of the choice options that already exist. Of course, in some poor urban areas the situation is quite different. Many schools in these areas have a myriad of problems that Jonathon Kozol (1991) spelled out in *Savage Inequalities*.

Some parents do choose schools based on appropriate criteria. Some believe certain schools provide a better sense of community, are more intellectually rigorous, or have better after-school activities or sports teams. How do they get information on the quality of education? Most people are not aware of the specific details of what schools do on a daily basis. This is problematic because schools can be subject to a reputation based on unsubstantiated gossip.

Parent involvement

The desire to increase parent involvement was listed as a common goal for both advocates and opponents of choice. Although public schools may not want parents to have the power to dictate curriculum, most want to increase parental involvement. This is also true of choice schools. Many professionals seek a balance between the power of the parent, the administration, and the teacher. It is an interesting contradiction that choice advocates want parents to have more say in school governance, but parents are probably more involved and have more power in wealthy neighborhoods where their children go to good public schools, not choice schools. They have power because they have cultural capital. In other words, parents in those areas are academically, financially, and culturally part of the mainstream.

On the other hand, in private schools, although the parents pay for tuition, they may not have quite as much voice in school operations. This is true especially in religious schools where people may simply trust the clergy to provide appropriate education for their children, and indeed believe it is inappropriate to question them. So, practically speaking, parents could have a lot of control in a public school or little control in a private school. Schools can work to encourage parental involvement whether or not they are public or private.

Magnet schools

Since people historically have not taken advantage of their choice options, school personnel have developed strategies to entice people to go to schools in different neighborhoods, particularly through the use of magnet schools. They frequently stand out as being different or better than other schools, and local authorities may use the concept to address ethnic disparities as much as to provide an enriched curriculum. The distinctiveness of a magnet school is well marketed to the public so that, for example, if parents and children want to focus on math and science content, they may choose a magnet school with this emphasis, although, as at Thomas Jefferson High School for Science and Technology in northern Virginia, the competition between students to be selected for the school is intense.

An example of a successful choice program with extensive parent involvement was implemented in Harlem. This reform effort started in a little school in Central Park East. There administrators, parents, central office personnel, and many other constituents wanted to do something about the failing schools in poor areas in New York. They used various strategies such as developing mini-schools that were housed within one building. They also had supportive school administration and strong and supportive leadership in the central office. But those who talk about the success in Central Park East emphasize the importance of choice and parent involvement (Fliegel and MacGuire, 1993; Meier, 1995). Schools that were failing were eventually closed down as parents started choosing better schools for their children. Soon, new, better schools sprung up, and old, ineffective schools were shut down.

V Formulate the shared problem

Define the problem and decide on a course of action

Here is a summary of some of the questions that emerged from our analysis:

The free market and the improvement of schools:

- What type of "choice options" will be most effective in improving education?
- Who should have control of the schools, administrators, teachers, parents?
- What type of governance structure supports school improvement?

Issues of race and class:

- Does choice perpetuate class and race segregation and stratification?
- Do public schools perpetuate class and race segregation and stratification?
- Do public schools or choice schools eliminate class and race segregation and stratification?

Parental involvement:

- Should parents decide for their children which aims of education should be emphasized?
- Can all parents make informed choices about schools?
- How can we make information available to parents about school choice?
- What happens where parents are not interested in their children's education?
- Does choice improve parent involvement?

Financial issues:

- Should the public pay for vouchers for public schools?
- Should the public pay to have children go to religious and other types of private schools?
- Should the public pay for inter- or intra-district transportation costs?

Democratic responsibility:

- Will school choice destroy neighborhood schools? Will it destroy our sense of community further?
- Is it our democratic/moral responsibility to work to improve public education for all? Do we have a moral responsibility to allow people to choose?

To define the problem, we refer to our list of priorities. At the top of our list, we have as our first question, "how can we improve the quality and the opportunity of education for disadvantaged students?" This could be one possible shared problem. At this point, the advocates must consider the options and decide for themselves which problems need further analysis. Considering our long list, this issue needs careful consideration in an extended reconciliatory conversation.

Reflection and speculation

With the Connected Math example, we found advocates on both sides who claimed expertise in teaching mathematics. It seems likely that these people could come together and use their expertise to develop a new approach. For competition and collaboration, we found that using both strategies and addressing the concerns of competition seemed a likely option. Perhaps people should compete in cooperative situations.

Where we have discussed competition and collaboration and the Connected Math controversy, the similarities and differences were comparable in number. For choice, however, the differences far outweigh the similarities. We don't find a lot of practical inter-relationships as we did with competition and collaboration. The differences are not myths that seem to polarize the oppositions way out of proportion. With choice, people have very different ideas about how schools should be governed. Also, people use statistical evidence to support their positions. This research evidence has been batted back and forth to support several arguments with no discernible effectiveness. One group presents statistical evidence and the other disputes the validity of that evidence. Then the first group disputes the validity of the statistics that shed doubt on the validity of its statistics and the cycle perpetuates itself. This is a good example of how people can find social science research evidence to support different positions. With the choice controversy, it is quite likely that a compromise might be the best option available.

To speculate on the outcome of further analysis of this opposition, we first must ask ourselves: Is it possible to take choice away from parents who have already experienced this option? Does anyone really want to force parents to send their children to schools considered dangerous or educationally bankrupt for the good of a democratic society? On the other hand, should private businesses control our schools? Stated like this, the oppositions are being unfairly polarized because we are not taking into consideration private schools, which are already a type of business. So the question then becomes: "How can we create a common problem through building on the best of both arguments?" First, let's take a look at some of the best features of both arguments keeping in mind this is a subjective process that would have to be decided in a reconciliatory conversation:

How do we rank these choice options?

- Motivation for improvement.
- Freedom to choose.
- Ability to integrate children when neighborhoods are segregated (better option than forced busing).
- No fear of government and bureaucratic malaise (support for entrepreneurial innovation).
- More parent involvement in school decision making.
- Local school personnel will have more freedom to "do what is best for their children."

How do we rank neighborhood schools options?

- Dedication to community.
- Making sure all children receive equitable education.
- Less stratification.
- Inability to segregate when neighborhoods are integrated.
- No fear of capitalist monopoly.
- Bureaucratic structures are in place to make sure people are treated fairly.
- No fear that children will be turned away (e.g., special education students).

In practice most people have taken a moderate approach to choice. So far no American school district has committed to the free market. Yet choice options have been implemented in a number of districts and states.

So, what constitutes a good compromise? Brighouse (2000) tells us that the interests of the children should be paramount in guiding our decisions as to how to design educational institutions. He emphasizes the children's interest in becoming an autonomous adult, and the interest in equal opportunity. Yet presumably few would disagree, as the devil is in the details. This demonstrates once again that policy decisions may be based on balanced arguments, but those arguments have also to be rooted in a person's or a group's ideas about what aims of education should be emphasized. It seems some type of controlled choice would provide the best compromise available. This option calms the fears of people who don't want public schools to be at the mercy of the free market since a democratic body is overseeing the schools and making sure that we adhere to lofty ideals presented by our American forefathers. On the other hand, controlled choice gives poor parents some alternatives. They are no longer forced to send their children to schools they believe to be inadequate.

Compromise can be disappointing. With compromise, it is often necessary to take away something important from each constituency group as part of the solution to appease a majority of people. By the time we are done compromising, nobody is happy, but most are satisfied enough to move on, recognizing the need for compromise in a democracy. When we compromise, we can end up with what some call the lowest common denominator.

In the case of choice, however, it seems likely that we cannot yet define the problem properly because there is too much speculation and not enough evidence. We could seek to build on the best of both arguments and come to a compromise that would take advantage of the best features of both options. Of course those who advocate for complete freedom of the market will not be satisfied, and those who believe we should develop community around local schools will not be happy either. But the kind of evidence needed, in this case for controlled choice, is illustrated in the following example.

This promising example of a controlled choice school system is provided to us in Lowell, Massachusetts (Young and Clinchy, 1992). Lowell has an intradistrict plan. It has open enrollment within two attendance zones. These zones are carefully considered based on specific geographic areas of the city, traditional school flow patterns, bus routes, and the ethnic and racial balance of the district. Applications for all schools (except the high schools) are made through the Parent Information Center (PIC). The PIC admits students to individual schools based on a number of criteria, often associated with the ethnic or racial makeup of the school district. The PIC makes an extraordinary effort to reach parents. For example, it has bilingual parent liaisons available who can speak a number of languages.

When parents register children, they list their first three to five choices. They can choose schools within their zone as well as two city-wide magnet schools. Approximately 70 percent get their first choice, and 97 percent get one of their top three choices. Afterward they are put on a waiting list and can move to their first choice school when a slot comes open. Students are admitted to schools according to a number of criteria including space availability, majority and minority balance, sibling preference, and closeness to home. The implementation is quite complex and therefore Lowell's controlled choice option is expensive. Parents who do not get their first choice can appeal to a parent-run review board and transportation is paid for by the school district. Parents choose schools according to a number of criteria. Some examples include newness of buildings, condition of playground, existence of hot lunch, whether it is K-3 or K-8, availability of all day kindergarten or latchkey programs, closeness of the school to the parents' work-place, etc.

In an attempt to attract children away from their neighborhoods, Lowell also provides a magnet program and many of these schools focus on writing, or computers, or the arts, etc. They also have two city magnets, one is called Arts Magnet and one is called City Magnet. City Magnet is very popular. It calls itself a micro-society school and learning is structured under that frame of a city management system. Children have different jobs. In publishing they have year-book, newspaper, gossip magazine. In economics they have stationery store, banking, holding company, primary store, and crafts (to name a few). They have a mini-government that decides upon student punishments, etc. Children pay taxes to support their government. The waiting list for this school is quite long.

The controlled choice as described in Lowell has been reported as being successful for a number of reasons. First, racial and ethnic balances have improved. Prior to the choice implementation these parents had some schools that had 90 percent majority and 70 percent minority. Now the schools are better integrated. They associate higher test scores, and therefore academic improvement to choice reform efforts. They also believe that the controlled choice has institutionalized parent participation. Finally, controlled choice in Lowell has increased the involvement of principals and teachers in program development and implementation. In their book on school choice, Young and Clinchy (1992) credit Superintendent George Tsapatsaris for a great deal of the success in Lowell. They describe him as a man who is interested in parent, teacher, and principal involvement in curricular and instructional reform (p. 81).

Lowell seems to provide us with an example of building on the best of each argument. There are enormous difficulties in this model and certainly it doesn't work perfectly. It is acknowledged in the literature that some schools in Lowell are still "better" than others and educators are working to make sure all the zone schools are made "equal." They do not, however, have students admitted to certain schools based on testing or some other type of filtering device. All students are admitted to different schools depending on the criteria listed above. In this city, they seem to be reaching out to achieve the goals set forth for choice, while also being cautious to address the concerns people have about choice. Both sides of this debate might consider whether Lowell is indeed a good example of common ground. If not, they may stand outside the framework for RD on this topic. One major part of the evaluation of schools, as shown in this chapter, is testing, itself the topic for the next chapter.

7 How should children's learning be assessed?

The testing controversy

Since we have all been to school, we have taken all kinds of tests, often without knowing why. Tests are as much a part of the framework of schooling as desks, books, and teachers. When Hugh was a child, intelligence tests were used in English state schools to sort children according to their abilities. By the time a child was 11, it had been decided by examination whether s/he would go to a grammar, technical, or modern school. Then, of course, children were sorted again as teenagers because those in the grammar schools competed seriously for positions in the top universities. Other children, like Hugh, who went to boarding schools, competed for acceptance into the most prestigious boarding schools. When Pamela applied to Ph.D. programs in the United States, the first question asked of her in every interview at every university (sometimes before asking her name) was: "So what did you get on the Graduate Record Exams?" For Hugh, tests were mainly comprehensive. He doesn't recall ever taking a multiple-choice bubble test. Pamela rarely sat examinations of any other type.

Although proponents of testing emphasize the importance of assessing children's learning, when we think back to our personal experience of testing, the realities of being sorted according to "ability" is what we remember most vividly. As far as authentic assessments are concerned, most adults would claim their teachers never used authentic assessments. This is probably not true. It is quite likely that your shop teachers made you sculpt table legs, your PE teacher had you run that mile around the track, your foreign language teacher forced you to recite a dialogue, and your English teacher expected you to write a formal essay. We were all assessed in different ways, but what we remember most is the paper and pencil tests.

In this chapter, we take a look at the controversy about whether we should use testing or authentic assessments. A practical example of this controversy might manifest itself in a school where half the teachers believe in giving children tests and the other half believe in using authentic assessments. This disagreement is dividing the school, pitting the veterans against the newcomers. The experienced teachers believe the new teachers don't listen to them and respect their expertise. The new teachers believe the experienced teachers are set in their ways and out of touch with new approaches. The veterans believe they have tried all the new approaches every time they cycle back in favor. The new teachers believe the experienced teachers have bad attitudes. Both sides become angry when policy decisions support one side or the other. These teachers obviously need a reconciliatory conversation.

I Locate the issues

Describe the oppositions and their origins

In their book about the effects of testing, Kellaghan *et al.* (1982) point to a number of references that demonstrate that examinations from ancient times to the present have been accused of being responsible for a wide range of societal ills. These authors point to literature that shows how in 1944, for example, people were blaming everything on tests from serfdom to defective art, to labor unrest, to mental defectiveness, along with the more common criticisms. In their own era, these researchers point to a 1976 newspaper commentary on standardized testing that blames the misapplication and misinterpretation of test results on injuring individual students, eroding curriculum and instruction, creating social and intellectual segregation, fostering elitism, fashioning a punishment and reward system, stigmatizing, and so on. In the 1990s, it is possible to still read newspaper articles presenting more of the same controversies and repeating the same complaints.

Phew! The controversy remains.

The issue of accountability

This emotionally charged controversy has its roots in issues of accountability. Over the decades, issues of accountability have been a driving force in educational reform. If the results of assessment procedures indicated that the system was failing (whichever of the three purposes is salient) then politicians and public searched for reforms to correct this dilemma. Often, standardized tests were (and still are) used for this purpose.

Standardized tests

A standardized test is one given under the same conditions to all students in a particular group. It presents the same questions to different populations in order to make comparisons between them. According to Mitchell (1992), it provides answers to such questions as:

- Is this child reading at a level comparable to others in the third grade in a different area?
- Are this year's students reading at a level comparable to students from last year or previous years?
- Is this district doing better than other districts?

Most tests are designed to show where a given student lies in comparison to a group of her/his peers. Test questions are not selected to establish how much that individual student knows of what s/he ought to know, but whether s/he is below or above the norm for her/his age and by how much. Tests with this kind of purpose are called "norm referenced." Equally there are tests that do seek to discover what the child ought to know at a particular stage of development or education. Rather than testing against a norm, the test is against a criterion (i.e., the knowledge the child should have), so tests with this kind of purpose are dubbed "criterion referenced" (see Gellman, 1995).

Authentic assessment

Authentic assessment focuses on individual students, not on comparisons. It is usually described as being analogous to the real world. It seeks to assess what students have learned in a context that is congruent with real-life experience. It can therefore include any number of methods used to gather information about the performance of students (among which might be both norm-referenced and criterion-referenced standardized tests). However, "authentic" assessment encompasses much more than testing. It regularly includes information on student performance, student products – often in portfolio form – and student attitudes or values (from Baron and Boschee, 1995).

Authentic assessment, we are told, is founded on two basic ideas: (a) that the purpose of education is to prepare students to complete life's relevant tasks and to use academic skills in concert to complete those tasks, and (b) that assessment must be matched to the principles of effective instruction.

The controversy surrounding testing and authentic assessment is not trivial. The questions embedded in the opposing positions have serious consequences for how our social systems have developed. We located the issue by describing questions out of which a theory and practice of assessing children's learning has grown:

- How do I (the teacher) know whether this child has learned what s/he has been taught?
- What kinds of tests (of any kind) can I (or someone else) give to the child to enable me (and others) to assess the child's learning exactly, and in comparison with other children?
- Should the test be part of the learning experience so that it can feed directly back into the child's understanding?
- How do I (the teacher) improve my teaching from the information about children's performances in testing (of any kind)?
- How can we organize the selection of children fairly and effectively for "X"? ("X" here could be college, a gifted program, a special needs program, etc.)
- Since the public hires teachers to have them teach children, how can the public be assured children are learning?

- As some schools do better in having children learn than others, which fair and objective tests can be given to indicate which schools are successful and which are in need of improvement?
- Can we get objective results from such tests to ensure that resources are fairly distributed?
- How can tests help us to discover general questions about the quality of children's learning (in a given state, school division)?
- Should there be, in any of these cases, many different kinds of tests?

These are the kinds of questions that people have confronted in the arena of educational testing and assessment, which give us the layout of the controversy in this tortuous area of education.

Hidden issues and surrogate problems

It is important to determine whether the debate about assessment is a cover for debate about educational purpose. Discussion about the relative merits of standardized testing and authentic assessment may hide more fundamental disagreements on the purposes of education in general. If so, we would find many people inaccurately comparing standardized tests to authentic assessment, using the differences between them to make broad generalizations about the differences between a traditional view of education (which they believe supports standardized testing) and a progressive view of education (which they believe supports authentic assessment). In our example of the divided teachers at the beginning of the chapter, it is quite likely their controversy goes beyond assessment.

It is important to keep in mind that people in power control testing. Children take tests. College students take tests. Job seekers take tests and people who want to join the military take tests. People who have power usually do not take tests. Those who make decisions about testing no longer have to endure the stress or the humiliation often associated with testing, and they decide what knowledge is valued. Testing is a filtering device, as Mitchell (1992) has pointed out to us, because it focuses the education process (when teachers teach to the test); it is also a powerful tool for imposing certain values on teachers and students. For example, the quest for school accountability became high profile after Sputnik was first shot into space in 1956, triggering all kinds of alarms about the quality of American education. It is possible that a conversation about standardized testing could be focused on the need for neighborhood schools to be accountable to parents, but a central issue is how those in power can enforce their educational priorities on the schools. As an extreme example, many Americans would like the United States to be considered the best in the world in scientific achievements. Some might go so far as to accuse the government of wanting to encourage children to be scientists and mathematicians so it can maintain its military superiority. If this were true, developing a filtering device that allows only those children who were exceptional in science and math to have access to the best schools and the best jobs would make a statement about what is valued. If you were engaged in RD on this topic, would you want the conversation to be about accountability or power and control of knowledge?

Another hidden problem to address with regard to testing relates to the fact that testing has become a huge business. We now have different and widely used achievement tests – the Iowa Test of Basic Skills, the California Achievement Test, the Stanford Achievement Test, and the Metropolitan Achievement Test to name a few. The National Commission on Testing and Public Policy (1990) estimated that students take 127 million separate tests in a year. Since there are 41 million students in American public schools, children take about three tests per year on average, over and above the regular classroom quizzes. The discussion could be affected by the fact that the decision to stop standardized testing could put a few people out of business! Perhaps superintendents should not hold stock in a testing company.

II Work out similarities and differences

Set out central values and outcomes

While standardized testing has been dominant, it has come under serious critique as a form of accountability. Some of the attacks on it quoted at the beginning of the chapter (e.g., defective art) seem somewhat extreme. Contemporary critics of testing voice complaints that are partly ethical (e.g., assessment should not be used to compare and categorize students, tests make students anxious and stressful), partly technical (e.g., standardized test makers control what students learn; test scores are inflated because of teaching to the test; standardized tests are biased against some students), and partly educational (paper and pencil objective tests measure only the most trivial learning). Because of these criticisms, the drive for authentic assessment has increased. It has been advertised as a way to gather richer information about student progress that moves beyond the static numbers of standardized tests (Shaklee *et al.*, 1997). Its advocates point to the diversity of children (by race, income, class, gender). It seeks a form of public accountability, which will do justice to that heterogeneity. The disadvantages of this type of assessment are high cost, difficulty in making the results quantifiable, objective, standardized, etc., and their lack of validity, reliability, and comparability (Baron and Boschee, 1995).

Similarities

All parties agree on the need for documenting children's progress. The overall purpose of assessment is for diagnosing student problems, making judgments about pupils' performance, providing feedback and incentives to pupils, placement of pupils, planning and conducting instruction, and establishing and maintaining the classroom social equilibrium (Airasian, 1997). While "documenting" and "progress" may be differently defined, under the best conditions and contexts, both portfolio assessment and multiple-choice testing can formally accomplish these goals.

- Both types of assessment can motivate teachers to think about what they really want to accomplish, obliging them to reflect on goals, methods, and individual child progress.
- Both can provide information that can be used to improve instruction.
- In principle, and subject to detailed examination, both could also motivate children, depending on the educational framework of the classroom. Teachers often use assessment procedures as a means to encourage children to study harder.
- Both believe the schools need some type of public accountability.
- Both sides agree that we need to improve the way we assess children's learning.
- Both agree that the overall purpose of assessment is for diagnosing student problems, making judgments about pupils' performance, providing feedback and incentives to pupils, placement of pupils, planning and conducting instruction, and establishing and maintaining the classroom social equilibrium.

Differences

We believe that there are at least three ideological differences: on purpose, objectivity, and types of information. We will examine each in turn. However, we need to remind people of our remarks about the need to be aware of both differences and perceived differences. The latter might not be justified as we dissect them, and they might not hold up under scrutiny, being simply part of an oppositional myth that embodies the debate.

Difference 1: purpose

One perceived difference between the generality of authentic assessment and of standardized testing relates to distinct purposes, even though there may be the formal similarities we have identified. Authentic assessment is credited with an educational purpose, to understand children. Standardized testing has a more administrative or bureaucratic purpose – to compare, sort, and classify.

We would like to emphasize that this is a perceived difference. A teacher could use either an exam or some type of authentic assessment to accomplish both purposes. For example, teachers could use portfolios much as they use tests to compare students. In the evaluation of portfolios and the assignment of grades to them, teachers could even use a normal curve of distribution to "score" the portfolios. The practical application of authentic assessment provides huge opportunity for co-mingling its purposes with those of multiple-choice testing.

Assessing what the student knows for the "sake of instruction" implies information not merely for the teacher, but also for the child and for the parent. In some cases, teachers have children construct portfolios and then specifically invite parents to read them regularly and enter comments, drawing the parent as a partner of some kind into instruction. Portfolio assessment is also instructionally cumulative. Students can retain portfolios as records of their work and they can build future work, developing intrinsic motivation in the child.

Just as the purposes of authentic assessment broaden within the educational context, so multiple-choice testing by a teacher could broaden its purposes and utility outside education. (Realtors will use publicized test scores to sell houses. School administrators will evaluate principals through test scores, regarding test score results as a measure of effectiveness.) Within the classroom, the purposes of multiple-choice questions could be manifold: for example, intensifying competition between children, constraining children's learning within what will be tested, motivating all children with extrinsic rewards, preparing them for the many kinds of multiple-choice tests they will meet later on, and so on.

In sum, while the purposes of each seem to be dissimilar, they can be mixed and used for intrinsic and extrinsic purposes in the practical context of the classroom.

Difference 2: objectivity

Multiple-choice testing is often considered objective; authentic assessment is considered subjective. Easier said than understood! What do we mean when we use the words "objective" and "subjective"? In a rough sort of way, we all know what they mean. When people say something is true (correct, right, or whatever) *objectively*, they mean that (a) it would be seen as true (correct, right, or whatever) by anyone who looked at it seriously, and (b) "it" is independent of whatever we happen to think. When we speak of something being subjective, on the other hand, we are emphasizing the person's particular experience or point of view, as when someone says they prefer Frank Zappa to Franz Schubert, or they like the chaos represented in the paintings of Jackson Pollock.

We as authors believe that the claims of all standardized tests to be objective underplay their potential subjectivity. We also believe that the claim that portfolio assessment is necessarily subjective underplays its potential objectivity. Neither is pure. As is sometimes said, "Macintosh computers are supposed to be easy and they're not. IBM computers are not supposed to be easy and they're not." This may be true of assessment strategies! Tests are supposed to be objective and they're not. Authentic assessment is not supposed to be objective and it isn't.

Advocates of testing (standardized or multiple choice) often promote the idea that the scores are a "true" (and objective) indication of ability. Results are fixed and unchangeable. They often take on more significance than they should, and they are often used and read as predictors of an individual's future. Tests present the illusion of objectivity, especially where they are used as public measures of the quality of a school, and a school board can use the "objective data" to show X is better than Y. These points about objectivity do not constitute, for us, an argument against using tests at all, but to understand their limitations and not to get overwhelmed by their apparent scientific expertise.

Even the argument that commercial standardized tests are put through a rigorous procedure in an attempt to attain objectivity is suspect. When we think of a group of corporate psychologists designing a test, they have to have some formal assumptions about the children or adults taking the test. Out there, as it were, is a "test taker" of a given profile. That profile implies that all who take the test share that profile. That is, the test takers are a homogeneous group, like those taking the driving test who, although they are wildly dissimilar in age, race, gender, and so on, for the purposes of the driving test, are a homogeneous group, namely intending drivers.

The notion of a homogeneous group of *test takers* simply may not match the heterogeneity of *children* in classrooms. Children can earn better scores on tests simply because they are well organized and well coached. Test takers may or may not be under stress, although where tests have a major potential impact on our lives (e.g., SATs) combating stress does become a significant part of the process, but one different for each individual test taker. The situations in which tests are taken and the mental and physical state of the individual test taker cannot easily in practice be taken into account, but must undermine the claim for objectivity. Everyone who takes the test is formally equal (i.e., they are all taking the test and the bare physical conditions are similar), but they are not all the same. This heterogeneity is, finally, not a matter of "stress or no stress," but speaks to other attributes of individual personality often negatively affected by the harmful effects of race, class, and gender inequities. To these common problems of standardized testing, a teacher devising her/his own tests could be sensitive, yet they are problems not shared with individualized portfolios.

Good tests are difficult to construct and require professional expertise (whatever one thinks of them ideologically). We have all taken tests where it was easy to choose the correct answer, whether or not we knew the information, because the "distractors" (the wrong answers) are simply ridiculous or inconceivable answers to the question. On the other hand, we have all taken tests where three of the answers might be correct and yet only one is correct. In truth, if a teacher designs a test, s/he decides what is important to know and why. S/he decides how to write the questions. S/he decides how many questions to present. S/he decides how many distractors to use. S/he decides how to score the questions. All of these would be her/his own subjective decisions. (Of course, sometimes the teacher setting such tests can play jokes on the students. A biology professor we know once set a multiple-choice question which involved asking 101 students how many legs a three-legged dog has. Over 10 percent of students gave an answer other than three, all of whom when asked thought the question was a trick.)

Turn now to portfolios. Unlike tests with assumptions of objectivity, portfolios are thought of as subjective in terms of the way teachers appraise them. To repeat, the objectivity of tests is overplayed and the potential objectivity of authentic assessment is underplayed. Why?

One person can judge a portfolio and others can confirm the judgment. This gives it more than just a subjective quality. In doctoral dissertations, for example, examiners judge non-subjectively and impartially, but not objectively. That is possible in the assessment of a portfolio. We know of teachers who have devised portfolio assessment procedures for children who wish to graduate from sixth grade (Almarode *et al.*, 2000). Not only are the children evaluated by the teaching team (four sixth grade teachers) but the teachers also have people from the community (superintendents, principals from other schools, college professors, community leaders, and others) come each year to go through these portfolios with each individual child. So, ultimately, at least five people are evaluating these children's portfolios according to a set of standards laid out by the teachers.

Difference 3: types of information

Tests are thought to provide quantitative data (numbers) and authentic assessments provide qualitative data (reports). Numbers are thought to provide objectivity and reports are thought to be subjective. The questions are what do the numbers tell us and what do the reports actually say? Test designers can do item analysis on test questions that produce useful reports of qualitative data from quantitative tests. Portfolios can be scored with numerical values.

Not all test data, therefore, has to be quantitative and not all portfolio data has to be qualitative. The real concern behind the "numbers issue" is that people believe that multiple-choice tests measure information that is almost exclusively connected to memory. In fact, the most ardent critics claim that multiple-choice tests measure only the most trivial learning because this is the type of learning that can be assessed with numbers.

Subsequently, to measure whether students can construct responses rather than simply recall facts from memorized textbooks, portfolios and other forms of authentic assessment can prove useful. The difference appears to be that while tests help teachers understand what students "know" about a subject, diverse forms of authentic assessment tell a teacher what the student can do as a result of knowing about the subject. However, it could be argued that if developed appropriately, some multiple-choice tests could be designed to test more than random facts. For example, if a test taker is asked to deduce the main point of the story (and is given a few plausible choices), this question requires a fair amount of interpretation.

Developing a multiple-choice test that can assess learning beyond facts is difficult, however. For example, a teacher may want a child to read some classic literature, and to somehow connect the story to her/his life and experience psychological growth. The difficulty inherent in trying to assess this type of growth is obvious. It is difficult to know whether or not a student has connected a piece of literature to her/his life and grown psychologically as a result. It is much easier to assess whether or not a student remembers the first name of the main character or can explain, for example, the moral questions posed in the story. Although good test developers might be able to design tests that go beyond facts, and portfolios may not always provide ways for teachers to assess psychological growth, authentic assessment would seem to take the evaluation process one step further. It seeks to determine whether teaching produces not only cognitive changes, but also affective changes in the learner.

One last difference to explore is that portfolios, as the example of authentic assessment, are considered more personal, because they invite the writer to discuss her/his views of learning, rather than to recapitulate the learning. A portfolio is a collection of work that represents more than domain-specific assessments. It is a personalized representation of the affective, creative, and other cognitive aspects of a student's personality. It is this that gives rise to the claim that different types of authentic assessment are more "personal," notwithstanding different understandings of the "personal." Clearly tests are impersonal, if only because the intent of the designer (whether teacher or corporate employee) is to see each test taker as just a test taker and marks of individualism are failures. The possible effect of different examination practices on individuals and social institutions has long been a cause for concern. People argue that traditional tests have shut certain populations, like women and minorities, out of opportunities.

In sum, the differences we have described (many perceived differences) are summarized as follows:

- Authentic assessment is credited with an educational purpose, to understand children. Standardized testing has a more administrative or bureaucratic purpose – to compare, sort, and classify.
- Authentic assessment would seem to take the evaluation process one step further in an attempt to determine whether teaching produces not only cognitive changes, but also affective changes in the learner.
- Testing is objective and authentic assessment is subjective.
- Testing provides quantitative data and authentic assessment provides qualitative data.
- A portfolio is a collection of work that represents more than domain-specific assessments. It is a personalized representation of the affective, creative, and other cognitive aspects of a student's personality. Testing measures domain-specific content.
- Authentic assessment procedures are less stressful to the learner. Testing is more stressful.

III Rank similarities in order of importance

Isolate the differences in which few have an investment and set them aside

So, if these oppositions share some similarities, and most of the differences are perceived differences, why is there so much controversy around this issue? Rather than list all the differences as we have in the last few chapters, we thought it would be helpful to locate a problem in a context, for contexts give rise to different discussions. Only in contexts, for this problem, can we determine what is important and what is not so important. Let us suppose that the problem is being discussed in a faculty meeting in an elementary school. Suppose that the staff are concerned because the details of test results have not been supplied by the state. Several parents have complained that their children's test results will prevent their graduation, and the faculty is divided on how far tests should be competitive, either between children or between classes in a school. Many children have started pressing for re-grades, and the PTA believes there is not enough of a reward structure, irrespective of issues of competition.

Rank the similarities in order of importance

Five questions now appear. We have tried to rank them as if we were teachers in the school:

1   Do test scores or portfolio assessments better help teachers know about students?
2   Are test scores used to help the teacher assess where children are in relations to their peers?
3   Are test scores used to shut children out of opportunities?
4   Are tests being used to motivate children to do better or are they being used to make children feel bad about their performances?
5   Are tests used to demonstrate to the class who is on the top or bottom of the curve?

Notice that we have moved to an array of problems that might emerge from a particular context, but to which our analysis of similarities and differences has contributed. The problem is now specifically located (in a school context), not generally located as we did with the broader controversy. It is now possible to see that most of the questions that are listed above are asking about how tests scores will be used. The controversy is not necessarily about tests, and it is not necessarily about portfolios, it is often about how test results are interpreted and used in practice. In a recent textbook for teachers and administrators, McMillan (2001) devotes an entire chapter to the topic of "fairness" and admits that to provide a thorough discussion of fairness in testing, he would need to write an entire book. While portfolio assessments could be used oppressively to make children feel bad about school, generally they are not used for this purpose. Similarly, testing has often been accused of being part of an oppressive process meant to categorize children, but it need not be used in this way. The true opposition here revolves around the uses to which we put the results of tests, not the methodologies themselves, and how these issues appear in a context of this elementary school, this class, these children, and these parents.

Three matters are immediately pertinent. First, the problems have been located in a context of a practical discussion. Second, each of these questions demands evidence for adequate answers, not just argument about ideology. In that sense they are capable of practical resolution, if the data is forthcoming. Finally, while we started with ideological discussion, we have arrived at practice (or context). But this shows that in every discussion about the practice of education, we have to use ideology to sharpen the discourse about practice, and every practical detail has the potential to shed light on the ideological.

IV Establish inter-relationships

Define mutual interdependencies

For the purposes of this chapter, while recognizing that context is important, we are going to shift back to the ideological, especially in terms of revealing inter-relationships.

Methodological complexity

To examine the methodological complexity, we must once again revisit the purpose of testing. According to a number of authors, authentic assessment is meant to add subjective, personal, and professional elements to the objective measure (Shaklee *et al.*, 1997). So, these people believe that authentic assessment should be used as an addition or supplement to testing. In fact, most of those who oppose testing would never claim that tests have no place in assessment. It is possible that an instructor might give a group of pharmacists a paper and pencil test that requires them to choose the appropriate medication (from a list of four choices) for a patient with certain symptoms. This is both a test and an authentic assessment. Few would argue that a paper and pencil test is not appropriate here. It is possible that the person could use real patients, diagnose a problem, prescribe medication, and then wait to see whether or not the patient lives. Most people would not recommend this assessment procedure, even if it were more authentic and would provide an effective learning experience. It might also seem more authentic if the person had to choose the medication from memory, rather than from a multiple-choice list. On the other hand, a multiple-choice test could be the first step among a sequence of assessment procedures. Also, many computer programs are available that can provide doctors with suggestions for prescribing medications. The point is that a multiple-choice test might constitute a fairly authentic assessment. Sometimes a teacher wants students to learn specific facts. For example, a statistician should know the statistical tools available to make the most appropriate choice of test for a specific problem. It would also be useful if that person could perform the appropriate test to analyze data.

Despite their apparent differences, testing and authentic assessment define two ends of a continuum. At either extreme there are subjects and people that may clearly be best evaluated with one method or the other. In between there is a large gray area. It is not hard to conceive of subject areas where a well-designed test might elicit some real insights into students' analytic and creative abilities. Conversely, there are certainly situations where an authentic assessment can reveal information about the depth of a student's factual knowledge.

Establish common educational practices – the old appeal

To establish mutual dependencies and practical inter-relations, we cannot ignore what happens in practice. We need a reality check. Why do teachers use one assessment form or another? Many would claim that teachers use tests because they are easier to give. Is it easier to give or take a test than to assess a portfolio or construct one? Anyone scoring a multiple-choice test is relieved of the burden of thinking since the correct answers are prescribed. However, developing a good test is not easy. It is said that multiple-choice questions in all their forms are supposed to be more difficult to construct if they are done properly. Does the teacher use the test over and over, or make a new test for every unit? Does the teacher spend time reworking test questions in an effort to eliminate non-discriminating questions? Does the teacher conduct item analysis after the test is scored? If a teacher puts a lot of effort into developing a good test, it could demand more time than quickly thumbing through a portfolio at the end of a semester, counting pages and grading on appearance. In reality, however, analyzing a test is probably a fairly rare procedure for a busy teacher and whether or not the teacher actually develops the multiple-choice test her/himself, or analyzes the results, portfolios certainly take longer to evaluate after the assessment has been delivered. Ultimately, whether they are more or less difficult to use depends on the reflective work that is involved in designing and analyzing the end products with either type of assessment. The practical reality is that most teachers think that tests are faster and more realistic given their time constraints.

Second, some teachers do not use portfolios because this assessment procedure includes the additional task of teaching children how to develop portfolios. Children know how to take tests. Children are taught from an early age that traditional tests are the most important form of assessment. They know what teachers expect from tests. They don't have to spend a lot of time figuring out "what the teacher wants," which is what most children focus on in school. When a teacher asks students to create a portfolio, the teacher must teach them how to develop a good portfolio. The teacher must teach them to critically analyze their work. The teacher must teach them how to reflect on what they have done and articulate their learning process. The teacher must face resistance from children who do not like ambiguity. These are wonderful teaching opportunities, but many people don't believe they have time to engage in this type of extra teaching because they need to concentrate on delivering instruction on specific content.

Third, parents don't always understand authentic assessment procedures. They do understand tests. And they expect their children to take tests. By using the traditional methods, teachers do not need to explain a new process and procedure to children, and they don't need to explain it to parents. Also, some parents want their children to take tests. They believe this will prepare their children for the reality of the test-taking world in which they live. Teachers face the challenge of changing norms and expectations as they use new forms of authentic assessment. Some don't choose to face this challenge.

Fourth, some people use tests rather than portfolios because they believe tests powerfully motivate children to learn. We are all conditioned to do well on tests. We study, we cram, we read, we pray, we do almost anything to earn high marks on tests. Authentic assessments certainly can be motivating, but they don't always bring about the same passionate response, unless the child is intrinsically involved with the material.

Often, it is the reality of the job that will determine the teacher's choice of method, not necessarily what the teachers believe is the best assessment. There is often a difference between the academics and the teachers. College professors may encourage teachers to "find a way" to do authentic assessment and dismiss the difficulties inherent in teaching, but teachers continue to use tests. College professors are not their employers.

Establish common educational practice – the appeal of the new against the old

Why then do some teachers use authentic assessments? Many teachers, administrators, and parents recognize the limitations of testing, especially in certain contexts, and for certain content. Teachers choose to experiment with new methods. They take risks. Often they are themselves transformed as a result of their experiments. Through authentic assessment, they develop a fuller picture of their children, they understand better how to address individual needs, and they use the results as data to improve their practice.

However, there are other reasons why teachers choose to move away from the traditional. For example, when teachers use constructivist methodology, it fits the contemporary model of a conscientious teacher. Teachers want to hear people tell them that what they do is good. Teachers are isolated in classrooms. Most of their wonderful innovations, their transformative lessons, and their patient redirections are appreciated by children, but rarely by colleagues, by administrators, or by parents. On the other hand, if something bad happens, they get a lot of attention. When a child puts together a portfolio, this represents not only the child's work, but also the teacher's work. In a job where there is little opportunity to climb the career ladder and earn status, teachers search for ways to demonstrate their professional excellence and their dedication to children.

In this section, we have shown how, when a problem finds a strong contextual base, numerous additional issues crowd into the agenda. It is thus an essential piece of RD to search for the overlaps and mutual inter-relationships between opposed positions.

V Formulate the shared problem

We warned you this would be a long haul, didn't we?

Define the problem

We have so far tried to show how the controversy is laid out, what the main terms mean, and taken a brief look at how things got like this. If we were discussing the problem of which is the most effective tool for public accountability, it would be difficult to compare the widespread practices of standardized testing with those of authentic assessment in general until authentic assessments are also used nation-wide. (Whether or not we should make nation-wide comparisons is a different, although related, controversy.)

Assessments vary according to their purpose, the type of behaviors they are intended to assess, the method by which information is collected, the degree to which the procedure is standardized, and whether they focus on individuals or groups. However, we could state the "real problems" as these possibilities, each showing where the oppositions lie:

1 What is the best way to improve public education? By and large, standardized testing proponents believe that it lies in tight control of schools and teachers, whereas advocates of authentic assessment believe that it lies in giving teachers autonomy and using other means of finding out whether improvement has occurred.
2 Which system can best provide public accountability of education? Both standardized testing and authentic assessment provide certain kinds of information, and they do so under the control of different agents.
3 How do we find "objective and fair" means of assessment for either 1 or 2 above? Standardized testing could be seen as "objective" and authentic assessment as "subjective," especially where individuals or groups feel penalized by such practices.

Decide on a plan of action

The definition of the "real problem" will depend on who is party to the discussion. Is it a group of school-board members, officials, teachers, or parents, or, of course, a mix of all four? It is possible that the real shared problem to be hammered out is *what should children learn?* After all, to come up with an appropriate assessment procedure, educators must first figure out what they are trying to teach. At this point, the protagonists need to decide on a shared problem among those we have listed (or from others) and either start to work toward a solution, or move through the discourse procedures again, narrowing the newly redefined problem.

Reflection and speculation

We found in our analysis that comparing standardized testing and authentic assessment was inappropriate because these two types of assessments are not used for the same purpose. Standardized testing is used for large-scale comparisons. Authentic assessment is used to assess learning in a specific context. If people wanted to compare local in-class testing to authentic assessment, this comparison makes more sense, but in that situation, we also found that many of the "differences" listed were not as "profound" or as "real" as many would have us believe. This opposition seems to be polarized out of proportion because of the personal (and therefore emotional) connection people have with standardized testing. We also found that testing and authentic assessment are difficult to compare because they are inter-related. People often use tests as part of authentic assessment procedures.

As an exercise in speculation, if people continued to work toward building on the best, our analysis so far would suggest that authentic assessment is "best" at helping teachers understand children's learning in most cases. This is especially true because authentic assessment usually measures skills that go beyond the memorizing of content-specific information. Testing is "best" to compare the factual knowledge of large numbers of children. For many proponents the question may be, "should children be compared in this way?" That question, stated as an opposition, could be taken through a reconciliatory discourse procedure if needed. If people agree that children have to be compared on a large scale, then much of what we know about education suggests that standardized testing carries with it a history of serious problems. To build on the best, we need to develop an alternative. Perhaps we could use what we know from authentic assessment to develop a better tool for comparing large groups of children, a tool that addressed concerns about testing. Linda Darling-Hammond *et al.* (1995) tell us that some states are already experimenting with authentic methods of comparison. They are using portfolios and performance assessments where (for example) children must perform science experiments. If we can't do that, we need to live with the best that we have – standardized testing. With authentic assessment, it seems educators should use authentic assessments to assess student's learning in classroom situations whenever possible, but we also need to address problems associated with the practical concerns of teachers. Not a surprising conclusion – teachers need time to teach well!

The difficulty with these arguments about testing is problematic in one major respect. Policy makers often want to use standardized tests to dictate the curriculum, leaving no serious room for authentic assessment as understood here. Yet there is no reason why a traditional curriculum, if that is being advocated by these policy makers, cannot be authentically assessed. So we need to first consider, "what should children learn?"

8 What should children learn?
Curriculum complexity

An answer to the question "What should children learn?" will describe the school curriculum. In this chapter, we take a reconciliatory *stance* to three curriculum issues: the approach to curriculum, sex education, and evolution and creationism in curriculum. We do not meticulously work through the five elements of the procedure with these topics, but RD does provide a guide to frame our discussion. In the following chapter, we seek to connect our educational insights, driven by RD, to matters of value and motivation with respect to educational purposes. The purpose of these two chapters, in other words, is to provide some food for thought for those engaging in RD, specifically on curriculum and its complexity.

What does it mean to take a reconciliatory stance in this discussion? Frankly, as we write, we are continuously tempted by the tricks of antagonistic debate and we have tried to sweep that particular virus out of our writing. Our main difficulty is posed by the mutual search for values and outcomes. Trying to describe views that we actually disagree with sympathetically is nevertheless essential if we expect to be involved in quality discourse. You will probably find the same experience as you try to shed the habits and attitudes of conventional debate.

Compulsory curriculum

At this time in our history, what children learn is mandated by the state. Jack and Garrett, like all other children, are compelled to go to a public or private school, and their parents are legally obliged to send them. If Pamela and David or Victoria and Greg wished to educate Jack and Garrett at home they must show that they are providing an education that conforms to a state's standards. Apart from the draft for the military and imprisonment, this is a real loss of liberty for both parents and children in a society that celebrates personal freedoms. Children are not merely compelled to attend but, with the exception of high school electives, they are pretty much compelled to learn what is set before them. Like countless other children, Jack and Garrett will hear from their parents that they are going to school for their own benefit. Yet it is not merely the children who benefit. At rock bottom, children must be civilized and socialized if a society is not to be threatened, as roaming gangs of street urchins in some of the world's cities as fictional stories like Doris Lessing's *Memoirs of a Survivor* remind us. At its height, the ambition is to have every member of a democratic society educated to make careful judgments about the future and shape of the country. But there is widespread disagreement about what children should learn.

To locate the question of what children should learn briefly, we describe three main areas:

- the subjects and topics to be taught;
- what should be taught at different levels of schooling (elementary, middle, and high schools); and
- the general purposes of education.

The subjects and topics to be taught

Should history and geography, rather than social studies, be taught? Should history teaching focus on heroes, politicians, and patriotism or on the complexity of social and economic history? Should elementary mathematics teaching be instruction in basic skills or getting children familiar with math concepts through ideas and play? Should science be useful? Should literature be chosen with an eye to conventional moral standards or should it help children cope with differences? These are familiar discussions and, of course, at different times particular topics erupt politically – creationism in Oklahoma, ebonics in California, and sex education most of the time everywhere.

Levels of schooling and what should be taught

People disagree about what should be taught at different levels of schooling, for example elementary, middle, and high school. Should a foreign language be available for children at elementary, middle, or high school level? What is the role and purpose of the kindergarten or Headstart programs? Should the content for such programs be determined by the elementary school or the social services? Are young adolescents "best" taught in middle or junior high schools? How is the high school learning environment unlike that of a community college? Should children be grouped by ability and not by age?

General purposes

So, people argue about what subjects should be taught and when they should be taught, but if asked to describe in general what children should learn at school, we would often get this kind of answer. At the minimum, children should be able to read, write, and speak English well, know something of the world's history and geography and their society, culture, and country's place in it, have a broad understanding of and competence in mathematics and science, and an appreciation of and familiarity with literature. They should also be mature in personal ways, understanding their moral agency and obligations as a citizen, as well as internalizing democratic principles. Other activities might be added for a well-rounded education, with recommendations for art education, driver education, ballgames and band, foreign languages and forensic debates clubs, sex education, and drama.

Not everyone sees the compulsory curriculum like this at all. The very way we write this list, for example as a general account of what children should know or be able to do, is immediately controversial. For it is opposed in many people's minds to their belief that what children should learn should spring from them, their interests and needs, from how they make sense of their world and its different meanings, not from the traditions of understanding which have marked the traditional school curriculum.

A third group would see both of these approaches to curriculum as irrelevant to the modern day. They are no good for training a person for economically productive citizenship. If these children are to get jobs, they need basic skills, they need to become team players, critical thinkers, problem solvers, and to be equipped with technological skills to enable them to contribute to society, their own economic future, and to take their place in the market economy.

You will recognize that old three-way division of purpose again – knowledge, self, and society. Any educational proposal is probably rooted in one of these three areas. In the following sections we want to take a reconciliatory stance to specific topics and categories of the procedure:

- student-centered and teacher-centered approaches to curriculum practice;
- sex education; and
- evolution and creationism.

Evolution and creationism present an interesting example. We intentionally chose to talk about this opposition because we believe that it cannot be reconciled. With teacher-centered and student-centered curriculum, we endeavor to locate the issues. With sex education we work to define the problem.

Approaches to curriculum practice: teacher centered and student centered

In this section we use a reconciliatory stance to describe and compare positions historically associated with a teacher-centered versus student-centered curriculum approach. A curriculum approach in our terminology describes the overall experience a child will have that a teacher has planned. The basic choice is this: a teacher (or whoever) could establish a body of content to be learnt through an established syllabus, or a teacher could decide on a general direction and allow the students' interests and concerns to shape what is studied. There are, of course, many other curriculum approaches, notably in a workshop setting where a master–apprentice situation defines individuals working at a task under the general supervision of the teacher.

Some elementary school children will experience a curriculum which is predetermined by the state, others a curriculum that flows in a general direction but is influenced by the teacher's and, more importantly, the child's choices. In a second grade classroom, for example, the predetermined curriculum in social studies might include "the early civilizations" (China, Greece, Rome). An alternative approach would be a curriculum that starts from Me (the child: who am I? where do I come from? my family), going out to Me and My Neighborhood. It would then progress to Me and My Environment (city or state or region), to Me and My World in which science, social studies, etc., would be included. With a predetermined curriculum, there would be weekly tests and prescribed writing for all children in the jurisdiction, and children would progress (or fail to progress) along the same lines. In an alternative curriculum, there would be projects and, depending on the teacher's ingenuity, all kinds of modes of learning, which could include dance, music, art, talking to Grandma, and reporting back. To assess these modes of learning, the teacher would probably have the students describe and document their experiences in a portfolio. For shorthand, let us describe the predetermined curriculum as "teacher centered" and the alternative curriculum as "student centered."

As we work to understand this opposition, let us explore some educational goals established by politicians in the early 1990s. When the Governors met with President Bush in 1989 at Charlottesville, Virginia, they announced six ambitious national goals for education, none of which have been realized. That is not for us a criticism, since we are advocates of a long-haul approach. They sought to improve standards and their work began the present strong focus on content. The first goal states that "all children should start school ready to learn." What does this mean? What do the schools expect?

The goal officially means that the basic mental and physical conditions are already established for the child to commit her/his serious attention to learning appropriate to first grade in a community of others of the same age. Schools therefore anticipate children being personally hygienic, understanding basic moral rules (like not gratuitously hurting other children), acquaintance with books of some kind, and an ability to cope in a community larger than their immediate caregivers or family. The school, the curriculum, and the first grade teacher formally expect all children to be responsive, eager, and competent, given the probability of different intellectual and attitudinal levels.

Yet many children, poor and rich, do not have these basic conditions with which to start school. Teachers who encounter classes with such children find themselves having to take the place of parents. (Presumably no one in a free society thinks that children should be taken away from their parents if they don't meet the standard, except in the most egregious circumstances.) Any adult knows perfectly well that not everyone can be a good parent and there are many other reasons than neglect or ill will for our weaknesses. So we also know that it is not the fault of the 5 year olds that they are "not ready to learn"; that is, dirty, unable to discipline themselves, accustomed to using foul language, aggressive, or silent and withdrawn. Since the child is not to blame, the teacher and the school morally speaking regard the child as a person who needs additional help and support. The moral ground for this includes the old notion of *in loco parentis*. It would seem the child needs a curriculum that is student centered, for, given the lack of "readiness" in the respects mentioned, the child is not "ready to learn."

Yet, not everyone would agree. Some advocates of a tough-minded teacher-centered curriculum would argue that there must be no concessions to such external forces. The teacher has some kind of stick (rather than carrot) readily available to quieten children who challenge teacher-centered curriculum through misbehavior. On this view, the teacher must not pander to background or be sentimental about children's contexts. Children must not be regarded as unable to cope. Set the expectations high and they will respond. Indeed they must be given the sufficient intellectual challenge guaranteed by the teacher-centered curriculum, just because they do not "start school ready to learn." Those children that fall behind are, it may be admitted, sad and deserving cases, but the curriculum is there to be followed.

In both approaches, the teachers may want to provide equity in educational opportunity and to address the child's lack of preparedness. But the teacher who is student centered might do so by focusing on providing extra help. The teacher-centered instructor might address background issues by setting high expectations for all children no matter what their background. Both have the same goal, but different approaches to achieving that goal.

For the purposes of RD, it is important to note that a significant shift has occurred in our discussion. We started by talking about curriculum approaches. Then we moved to the National Goals, embedded within which is the notion of equality of educational opportunity, exemplified by the statement that "*all* children start school ready to learn." "All" does not mean "some" or "as many as possible," or "the middle class"; it means what it says – all. The characterization of the strong teacher-centered view has shifted the discussion away from curriculum approaches and back to equality of educational opportunity. (Remember the quip of the old British judge who is said to have remarked: "The law, like the Ritz Hotel, is open to everyone.")

It is important to emphasize the connection between fundamental moral and political issues like equality of opportunity and curriculum approaches. The consequences that can result from the tensions between these two areas can be quite dramatic. For example, under the pressure of state testing, at least one superintendent in northern Virginia has told principals that the main thing is to have 70 percent of children pass the test to get the schools accredited. That presumably means that if much less attention is given to the 30 percent likely not to be good enough, so be it.

On the other hand, the interests and needs of smart children can be seriously disregarded in child-centered classrooms. Such children are expected to paint, draw, dance, and so on, when what they really want to do is sit in a corner and read or get on with long division. As with the teacher-centered example, the interests of the individual child are being placed second to the curriculum ideology. Because we ought to pay attention to the individual, we should notice that no one-curriculum approach can claim purity in this moral respect.

For the purposes of RD, this is a critical shift for a discussion: a major difference in an assumed area of moral agreement has been located and must be examined. If we put that shift of discussion to one side for the moment, however, the primary substantive difference between the student-centered and the teacher-centered curriculum seems to be a difference in attitude regarding the child's values and their development. The student-centered curriculum is based on the belief that what the child wants to follow, s/he should follow – without pressure to engage in activities s/he might not value. The teacher-centered curriculum is basically uninterested in the child's *existing* values, only that s/he is properly taught by educated teachers. The child is not required to like the curriculum, although this will, of course, be true for some children. We return to the topic of value in Chapter 9.

If we, as authors, were involved in a curriculum-approach discussion, the question of how to work with children who are not ready to learn would be very important. That reflects our commitment to a strong sense of equality of educational opportunity. We would also be interested in working with children on developing and understanding value. We would want to nurture their interests. We would wish, as a matter of urgency, to find ways to reconcile this stance with elements of the teacher-centered curriculum, and, for that matter, with the superintendent we mentioned.

To accomplish this goal, it would be important for us to listen to people as they shed light on these two approaches by probing the complexity of the topics. For example, we already know that the effectiveness of both the teacher-centered and student-centered classroom is greatly impacted by class size (Nye *et al.*, 1999; Grissmer, 1999). Between the ages of 8 and 13, Hugh was at a small private boarding school for 80 boys. Whatever its weaknesses (and they were considerable) he was never in a class of more than 15 children. Between the ages of 11 and 13 there were rarely more than 6 or 7 boys in his class. He had exceptional individual attention, whatever its quality, within a subject-based, teacher-centered curriculum. So while the curriculum was teacher centered in that no teacher was particularly interested in what Hugh thought about the curriculum as such, the teachers readily solved his individual struggles with the material on hand. At age 13, he went to a much larger school of 750 boys, in which he was expected to fend for himself and produce work, but not under such close supervision, a situation which he found difficult to cope with.

The point is this. However much we write about what children should learn, or about curriculum approaches, or the size of classes, we need constantly to bear in mind that the learners are children, whose experiences of learning are not just defined by the "curriculum approach." Being at school is what a person does for the first quarter of her/his life. As we grow older, our individual experience of schooling shapes what happens in our schooling. What the good teacher in Hugh's small classes could achieve was in fact exactly the kind of inter-personal concern and support typical of the student-centered curriculum, which Hugh then lost. To us, the radical diversity of these two curriculum approaches starts to diminish if we start by considering the child's perspective, the child's context, the child's motivations, and the values we wish to foster. Questions of the child's perspective on curriculum are therefore, for us, very high in any rank of importance.

Approaches to curriculum practice: sex education

And now for something completely different! Sex education provides some interesting challenges for those engaged in RD. Here we try to set out some similarities, differences, and levels of importance arising from it, which is itself a challenge as we seek to suggest how some of the problems of sex education may be defined. We choose not to use the euphemism of family life education.

Sex education is an interesting topic for us because it is so paradoxical. Few would argue that sex is unimportant in human life, since it is present in countless examples of human actions that can be sublime, ridiculous, or downright evil. Human sexuality is an integral part of literature, poetry, and art. Yet it presents a minefield for the unwary teacher. How does the teacher of literature handle King Lear's outburst "let copulation thrive"? Hugh once observed a young teacher in a classroom with a class of high school seniors who was so wary, shy, or timid that he taught the most intimate and erotic parts of *Romeo and Juliet* as textual analysis only! Sex forms an important sub-text in social and political history, and, of course, there's biology: say no more. Our sexual behavior is a part of our general moral behavior, involving matters of respect, the interests of others, and honesty at least. In any co-ed environment, finally, there is a continuing sexual politics, especially for adolescents struggling with their desires. Sorry, folks, but sex is here to stay and it's something we can't get away from in schools, however pure or puritan the ideal.

Sex education is not, as British philosopher Richard Peters (1966) pointed out, to be confused with sex training, which no classroom could contain (p. 34). As we have seen, while sex can be understood as just an animalistic pleasure, human sexuality interacts with all aspects of one's personal life and the lives of others. This, we think, would be a first important possible similarity for all sides in a debate about sex education. From it arises another similarity. Few people think that there should be no sex education for children, whatever view one has of its place in human life and even if parents won't take up the responsibility themselves, and independent, for the moment, of the frameworks in which it is couched. Here then are two similarities, important to establish in such a controversial field:

- Human sexuality is a complex part of human identity.
- Children should receive sex education.

There is one further obvious similarity. Sex education runs across the three educational purposes. That is, it clearly involves knowledge and can be enriched in terms of one's understanding through literature, poetry, and even in such famous biblical relationships as Samson and Delilah, and David and Jonathan. Manifestly it is highly individual as a form of expression, and it is important that children learn about social expectations and the constraints and opportunities for sexual expression within society. We need to explore issues of content, the limits to content, who should teach it, and the contexts children come from. All this, it seems to us, would be true from whatever point of view sex education is approached.

The content of sex education is controversial because it is so important to human beings. Debates continue about when sex education should start, about when children are "ready." Fairly early, if Jack and his cousin Abigail are any guide. For Abigail (then not quite 2) gave Jack a kiss (2½) when they were playing together over Thanksgiving, a fact that Jack reported with some disgust to his mother. The connections with love and matrimony are rarely gainsaid. Issues of content arise in co-ed schools where post-pubertal adolescents struggle with the new feelings of their sexuality, and, with girls now coming into puberty before leaving elementary school, what kind of sex education is important for them? Are people born homosexual, or is it a matter of choice?

The content is not just a matter of topics, of course. Can children be taught about sexual matters outside a moral perspective of some sort? Some would argue that children should be taught the "facts" as simply and clearly as possible. Yet where do these "facts" end? To what extent should they be taught the social facts about sexually transmitted diseases, comparisons of AIDS figures in different countries, and the complexity of disease that it brings? But if sex education is taught from a moral perspective, then how can we conjure agreement out of differing adult attitudes to, say, monogamy and fidelity? In curriculum terms, therefore, just as few would argue that sex education should be limited to technique (as in training) nor can it settle for just the facts without attention to the content of the complexities of human perspectives on sex.

Are there limits to what might be taught about, whether by parents or teachers? Are there, as Neil Postman (1984) puts it, some adult secrets which should be kept from children? Are topics like incest taboo, or just inappropriate even though some children are subject to assault from family members? Homosexuality is an aspect of human sexual behavior that arouses major controversy on how, if at all, it is to be dealt with in schools. Is it a good thing for children to discuss homosexuality? Yes, says the Gay Movement, both because some children experiencing homosexual orientations themselves need to be validated and because everyone needs to know about this feature of human desire. No, says the Religious Right, because homosexuality is a sin against God's law and even putting the possibility before children, religious or not, is implicitly to approve it and perhaps stimulate weaker brethren to be tempted into a homosexual adventure.

Who should teach sex education? Some parents regard it as their province entirely, whereas other parents hope they won't have to talk about it much, for they may be embarrassed, or ignorant, or resistant to being questioned themselves and having their teaching of it entangled with family emotions. Other parents believe it is none of the school's business, but not theirs either, suggesting it's the responsibility of the clergy. Teachers often prefer that it be the responsibility of counselors because they wish to be insulated from controversy. It is problematic for whoever does it. For, as if there aren't enough problems about understanding oneself sexually, how do I view myself as a parent or a teacher teaching, advising, or restricting children, with regard to masturbation, kissing, petting, dating, contraception, intercourse, or abstinence, indeed the whole litany of the teenage (and adult) life? And anyone posing as an expert, as educator or parent, can feel especially vulnerable because children, especially adolescents, will be inclined to speculate (if not directly ask) about the expert's sexual experience. Any volunteers?

Of primary importance for sex education are the different contexts from which children come. You would be forgiven for getting the impression from the media that teachers promote promiscuity. Yet most teachers we know are surprised and appalled by the precocity of many youngsters in sexual matters, though some now say they are not surprised by anything. Manifestly children talk about sex and learn from each other – for good or ill. Most teachers do not see a group of innocents before them, but a huge spectrum of differences of understanding and experience. For example, studying with us was a teacher who asked how a school should confront a mother who encouraged her 13-year-old daughter to be promiscuous. Or, another example: a teacher had been discussing homosexuality and indicating in decisive terms that she was "against it" at which a 12-year-old girl commented, "I don't like what you said. My mother is a lesbian." How does this teacher respond? Complicating everything are different ethnic attitudes toward sex, the respective place of men and women in differing cultures and sub-cultures, and what that implies for sexual behavior. Throughout these arguments are the recurring problems of the age at which children should be taught what, many of which are determined by the behavior that the children manifest.

Defining the problem(s) in sex education

We have isolated three very general similarities, but articulated a gamut of differences in four main areas. Assuming we were participants in RD, what problems might we suggest, defined in such a way that they offer potential for other participants to come together to reconcile their perspectives?

- What is the complexity of sex in human life that a child might understand through a curriculum by high school graduation?
- How does a common curriculum cope with the differences in the cultural and ethnic contexts from which children come?

- Are there common moral principles that we want children to follow in sexual relationships (e.g., honesty, respect)?
- Do we want children to come to regard sex as of intrinsic value?

These might be productive problems. Trying to articulate problems that people from different viewpoints can share is a central part of RD. But there are some cases, of course, where the controversy is just too deep.

Approaches to curriculum practice: evolution and creationism

Oklahoma's Divisive Disclaimer on Evolution
By Lois Romano
Washington Post Staff Writer
Wednesday, December 1, 1999; Page A03

TULSA, Nov. 30 – Oklahoma Gov. Frank A. Keating (R) has found himself in the middle of an education firestorm – not entirely of his making but which has nevertheless become a political embarrassment for him.

The brouhaha started last month when the Oklahoma State Textbook Committee mandated that publishers wishing to do business with the state place an unusual disclaimer on all new biology books, stating that evolution is a "controversial theory" that refers to the "unproven belief that random, undirected forces produced a world of living things."

The action by the committee – 11 Keating appointees empowered by statute to select public school books – was immediately excoriated by scientists and academics as misleading, and an attempt by religious conservatives in this Bible Belt state to promote a thinly veiled creationist agenda over science.

"Why would you appoint biblical literalists to a textbook committee and then be surprised that they want biblical doctrines substituted for science?" the *Tulsa World* demanded of Keating in one of three tough editorials on the matter.

Local and national science teachers' groups quickly urged educators to reject the lengthy disclaimer, and the American Civil Liberties Union of Oklahoma is considering whether the disclaimer as worded violates the First Amendment prohibition on the endorsement of religion. Science faculty members at the University of Oklahoma are in the process of drafting an open letter to Keating condemning the action.

And in Washington, Americans United for Separation of Church and State have warned the state in a letter that it is on shaky legal ground. "Having failed at their efforts to have creationism taught as a science in public schools, Religious Right activists are trying other strategies," wrote executive director Barry W. Lynn.

Meanwhile, about 700 teachers, parents and church members signed a petition praising the committee's stand.

Keating said that he was not a party to the committee's decision, but he has publicly supported it. At a recent news conference, he proclaimed that he doesn't think he is descended from a baboon, which prompted the *Tulsa World* to bluntly call Keating an "ass" on its opinion page. Under the headline "Gov. Gutless," the newspaper accused Keating of being "unwilling to stand up to those who would lead the state back to the stone age on this issue."

"It's much ado about nothing," said a clearly exasperated Keating in an interview this week. "We are not saying you must teach creationism in schools, or you must not teach evolution. We're saying be open-minded to all sides of the debate."

But critics maintain the disclaimer language distorts scientific theory for students who are just learning to think critically.

"To suggest evolution is controversial among biologists is simply untrue and it misleads students," said Michael Nunley, an anthropology professor at the University of Oklahoma. "It's only controversial as a political and religious issue among people who are committed to a different way of looking at the origins of life."

In addition, legal experts question the constitutionality of the disclaimer. The Supreme Court has consistently invalidated statutes that advance religion in public schools. In 1987, the high court struck down a Louisiana "balanced treatment" statute that prohibited the teaching of evolution unless accompanied by the teaching of creation science.

Keating has been a popular two-term governor, but he cannot run again. As the chairman of the Republican Governors Association, he was an early supporter of George W. Bush and helped mobilize support from fellow governors. The flap comes at a time when Keating is hoping for a Cabinet post in a potential Bush administration.

A Roman Catholic, Keating said that he believes in evolution, but that he also believes that somewhere along the way "man was infused with a soul – and that is not inconsistent with my religious belief." He said he does not believe teaching creationism should be banned in public schools. He called the disclaimer "thoughtful," but added that it may be "too broad."

The textbook committee, made up of elementary and high school teachers, is charged by state mandate with screening textbooks for Oklahoma's 540 school districts, which then may purchase only approved books from specific publishers. In appointing the committee, Keating bypassed the state's largest teachers union, the Oklahoma Education Association, in favor of members of the more conservative Association of Professional Oklahoma Educators.

It remains unclear whether the committee has overstepped its authority in mandating such a disclaimer. But barring a legal challenge, publishers will be forced to adopt the disclaimer to remain on Oklahoma's approved textbook list.

Committee member John Dickmann, a middle school teacher from Broken Arrow, Okla., said he introduced the disclaimer – identical to one adopted in Alabama – because the committee believed that textbooks rely too much on teaching Darwin's theory of evolution.

"We wanted to send a message to textbook companies that we want a more unbiased viewpoint," Dickmann said. The teacher insisted that for him the decision had "no religious overtones." However, at least one other committee member has said that her intention was to give creationism an equal voice in public school teachings.

Caveat for the Classroom

The Oklahoma State Textbook Committee has mandated that publishers who wish to do business with the state must include a disclaimer in their biology textbooks stating evolution is unproven. Here is an excerpt:

* This textbook discusses evolution, a controversial theory which some scientists present as a scientific explanation for the origin of living things, such as plants and humans.

* No one was present when life first appeared on earth. Therefore, any statement about life's origins should be considered theory, not fact.

* The word "evolution" may refer to many types of change. Evolution describes changes that occur within a species. (White moths, for example, may "evolve" into gray moths.) This process is microevolution, which can be observed and described as fact. Evolution may also refer to the change of one living thing into another, such as reptiles into birds. This process, called macroevolution, has never been observed and should be considered a theory. Evolution also refers to the unproven belief that random, undirected forces produced a world of living things.

Commentary

The 1999 Oklahoma controversy sharpened the clash between "secular science" and "dogmatic religion." "How did the world begin?" is an important question for children to grapple with in school. We need some clarifications as a way of defining the problem, though we recognize our clarifications may be seen as obfuscations by advocates. Let's try.

Up to the middle of the nineteenth century, most people brought up in a Christian tradition thought that God created everything that existed. They disagreed then, and still do among themselves, on the extent to which the Bible, including the Old Testament Book of Genesis, provides a literal detailed historical account of God's six-day masterpiece. Some Christians follow the traditions of the early church (i.e., during the 500 years after the death of Christ) and see the various scriptures making up the Bible as containing a general historical truth embodied in the life of Jesus as prophet in the long tradition of Hebrew prophecy. These Christians see the Bible, especially since

Saint Thomas Aquinas, as revealing the truth of God's existence in various ways, historical and factual, metaphorical and aesthetic, emotional and prophetic. Literalist Christians, on the other hand, believe in the literal truth. In 1654 Bishop Ussher famously calculated back from the birth of Jesus through the varied lineage of Jewish kings and prophets and declared that in the year 4157 BC God created the world in six days. This literalist view of the beginnings of the world was clearly put at risk when Charles Darwin set out a theory of evolution in his book *The Origin of Species* in 1859. Darwin and Lamarck, to whom Darwin constantly reiterates his indebtedness, represented a fundamental challenge to the literalist view of the doctrine of the Creation. We need to give an account of what that challenge amounts to, which, we hope, is fair to both the community of biologists and literalist Christians.

J. B. S. Haldane remarked that we should see "the problem of evolution" as not one problem, but three problems (You see? Define the problem). (1) Is it a *fact* that evolution has occurred? (2) If evolution has occurred, what is the *machinery* by which it works? (3) If it has occurred, can we discover any general rules to describe it, or find any main trends in the process?

What, exactly, is the fact?

> It is now universally held by competent biologists that all organisms, living or extinct, have arisen from remote common ancestors by a process of gradual change or evolution, and, further, that living matter or "life" itself, in all probability arose from non-living matter in the first stages of this evolutionary process.
>
> (Haldane, 1947, p. 917)

Scientists in general further argue that evolution is the backbone of chemistry. The elements must be created in the bowels of the stars. The universe was once just a seething cauldron of hydrogen. Gravitational forces, then electromagnetic forces, and finally nuclear forces combined to produce, through fusion, other elements. It required, however, the cataclysms of exploding stars to produce the very heavy and rare elements. Therefore, physics too has its foundation in evolution. These facts, for which there is no counter-evidence recognized by scientists, is used as a *theory*: that is, a framework of understanding through which data about fossils or the chemistry of life can be understood. The doubts about this theory in the minds of scientists, Haldane concludes, are *only* the exact steps in the process and the nature and relative importance of the various factors contributing to it; that is, the second question about the machinery. The creationists' beliefs, on the other hand, are based in faith.

The literalist doctrine of the Creation is that God created the world and particularly man in His own image in a certain order and within six days. (Whether "days" are to be thought of as 24-hour periods or not is often debated, but to debate it begins to sap the claims of the literalists.) Clearly, that view is incompatible as a literal truth with the fact of evolution as described above. One way of reconciliation, unsatisfactory to both science and literal

Christianity, would be to say that evolution has proceeded since the Creation, but by definition could not have *preceded* it. And this is what non-literalist Christians could comfortably believe. That is, they believe in God as the prime Originator, but they regard the Book of Genesis as an interesting and powerful story told as an allegory to a largely illiterate people who thought in images.

The machinery (Haldane's second question) of evolution is constantly being explored. Much of our understanding of changes in the contemporary world could not be explained without some concept of natural selection, of the chemistry of life, and so on. This theory of evolution is, on the scientists' accounts, the only rational view to take from the mountains of evidence from fossils, the chemistry of life, the patterns of heredity, continuation and perpetuation, and the struggle for existence characteristic of human beings and other living things. But what does it show about the literalist view of the Creation?

Its significance for literalist Christian belief (and for other similar religious positions) is more limited than is generally supposed by literalist Christians. While it is in clear conflict with the date to be assigned to the Creation, literally understood, because of (a) the element of time and (b) the notion of man being sprung into existence in God's own image, the fact and theory of evolution does not, and could not, prove that God does not therefore exist. Nor does it prove that He was not the originator of the universe. For such religious claims are simply *outside scientific proof* as generally conceived, even by those like Sandra Harding (1991) who are critical of the development of science. Scientists have not claimed and would not claim that God does not exist – on scientific grounds. They would say that the overwhelming volume of data provided in the world (whether by God or by nature) does not match up with the literalist Christian account. It is also presumably important for literalists to consider whether, notwithstanding the belief in God as creator of the world in six days, there has been evolution consonant with Darwinian and Lamarckian theory since that date. Is the objection to evolution, in other words, both pre and post creation, or only pre?

Given the religious, dissenting, and fundamentalist character of Christianity in the United States and the notion of freedom of conscience on which it was built, it is hardly surprising that the debate has simmered and sometimes exploded into the schools and the curriculum.

The problem, if defined by the literalist Christian view, is outside reconciliation.

For a person cannot believe that God made the world in six days and created man in His own image *and* believe that our world has emerged from a remote ancestry of non-living matter.

A person can believe in God as the originator, however far back in time that puts the Creation, and see the facts of evolution as part of God's intricate and marvelous handiwork.

But that would not be a literal statement.

Yet the schools we are talking about are public schools, not those owned by a sect, however committed, thoughtful, and principled. The creationists' beliefs carry no weight when we consider whether evolution should be taught in schools. It is quite another question as to whether the story of the Creation, as understood by literalist Christians, need be taught in schools. These two issues should not be linked intellectually.

The reconciliation process

We find it difficult therefore to define a problem to be shared by the world's scientists and literalist Christians, so that there could be some hope of reconciliation. We have pointed out that literalist Christians do not accept pre-Creation evolution – and we have not found any evidence of what they believe happened in the past 6,000–10,000 years by way of evolution.

Yet if we examine the conflict under the aspect of the ways in which children might come to value things, a different interpretation arises. For, in order for children to come to an understanding of value, they must also encounter how and why other people have found things of value. It can be argued that the religious motive in individuals has been and is very powerful and that, putting on one side the issues of church and state, we cannot comprehend much of the modern world without some kind of religious understanding. Opening up the curriculum to encounters with the spiritual aspect of humankind will seem to many an invitation to the desecularization of schools, to schools dominated by different religions, even cults that call themselves religions, often under the domination of some charismatic or evil character.

The problem then becomes whether children can encounter this aspect of humanity without being proselytized into a specific set of religious beliefs. Between evolution and creationism, however, there do not seem to be any ideological similarities at either a theoretical or a practical level. The differences are too great in terms of perspective and language. There are no decks to clear. What we therefore face, in our view, is not whether evolution should be devalued as scientific fact from which a theory springs, but whether the Christian notion of the Creation should be encountered by children – taught seems too strong a word – in schools.

9 Similar problems in the world of educational purpose

Some people may conclude that the ideas presented in this book are too idealistic. We agree they are idealistic, but we don't regard that as a criticism, given the ingrained habits of antagonistic discourse. Indeed, whether our proposals are valuable or not, sometime we have to find ways toward reconciliation. The difficulties inherent in changing the approach to educational controversy became very obvious to us the first time we experimented with the RD procedure in a class simulation with practicing teachers. In a full-day class session, we set up a debate in the morning, typical of what teachers are used to experiencing in class. The debate was centered on a problem of re-districting, which involved issues of race and class. The debate was about whether poor inner city school children should be bused to some suburban schools while their neighborhood schools were being refurbished. In the morning we simulated a school-board hearing and groups of students were asked to present the different perspectives associated with constituency groups. In the afternoon, the teachers were expected to "do the conversation differently" and try to reconcile the issues.

The teachers enjoyed the morning activities better and the reason seemed to be because they were accustomed to presenting opinions and trying to persuade. This exercise was easy and fun. In the afternoon, they found struggling together to define the problem and develop a solution tiring and frustrating.

Throughout the day, it became very apparent that teachers were used to arguing in a certain way. They were used to presenting their opinions, and although they listened to other people, the emphasis was on judging the quality of the presentations, not the quality of the arguments being presented. The strength and validity of the arguments seemed to be secondary. A few of the simulated board members (the students tasked with making the final decision) said after the debate that they were frustrated a few times waiting for someone to present certain arguments. They knew the arguments, they were simply waiting for them to be set out on the table so they could use them to support their positions and justify their decisions (see comments about public officials, page 73). All the groups seemed completely satisfied to let "the governing body" take responsibility for the final decision, although some may have been slightly annoyed that they didn't "win."

When asked to use the RD procedures, people did not like having to take a slow route to talking about the topic. They all wanted to offer solutions right away without investing sufficient time to thoroughly define the problem. A few people in one group complained that someone in their group kept trying to pull everyone into a conversation about race (which was a strange response because the exercise was about race issues). The people in another group were really frustrated that after analyzing the problem, they realized they couldn't come up with an answer, only more questions. One group of people had trouble following the procedures and kept on with their (very polite) antagonistic debate under the "categories of reconciliation."

That early experience made it clear to us that to engage in RD, people needed to have a clear understanding of the conditions, commitments, requirements, and procedures before starting the process. We needed a protocol. It was also obvious that we needed to emphasize that this process is a struggle, both because *it is* a slow and meticulous process that takes trust and struggle, but also because people need time to change the way they do business. An essential part of our invitation in this book is a reminder that we need to light a candle called patience if we are to figure out how to change the discourse on the basis of which policy decisions and the lives of countless individuals are determined.

Although this simulated debate was focused on a policy issue dealing with race and class and very different from the issues we have dealt with so far in this book, once again the argument was about purpose and motivation. On one side of the debate, people were arguing that it was important for inner city children to improve academic achievement (knowledge) so they could compete successfully in our society (extrinsic reward). On another side of the debate was the idea that children should be nurtured in a caring neighborhood community (self). Other groups argued that integration, although difficult to implement, would ultimately benefit everyone (society). They argued that integration was intrinsically motivating because through integration children learn the value of diversity.

Three main thoughts occurred to us as we explored curriculum and policy issues from a perspective of reconciliation:

- Educational practice frequently reflects all three aims.
- The division in educational purposes is now of historical interest only since attention to all three is necessary in a complex democratic society.
- Matters of how children get a sense of *value*, and thereby how they are motivated, indicate that each purpose embodies an important general educational experience.

The potential for integration

Our first thought is that it is possible for the three educational purposes to be integrated and complementary. Kieran Egan's (1997) book *The Educated Mind* is built around the claim that these purposes are incompatible and he develops a new conception of educational purpose. The problem here is, we believe, that the fundamental purposes are so engrained in people's expectations of education that, for public debate and private judgment to be coherent, the three purposes have to be the practical starting point. Much depends too on how individuals interpret them. Incompatibility seems to imply for practice that, if a system is a full-blooded embodiment of one purpose, then elements of another cannot be included. We disagree. We believe an educational *system* can contain important *elements* of all three at once.

What do we want for Jack and Garrett? For us, it would be very unsatisfactory if their educational experience K–12 did not contain major elements of each educational purpose. We are attracted as individuals by a public education encompassing all three. We want teachers to treat and nurture these boys as individual persons throughout their education, paying careful attention to their talents, interests, and needs. But not exclusively. We also want them to have access to the most important aspects of human knowledge, and to be taught by teachers who know their stuff. Yet we certainly want to see them properly prepared for citizenship and productive social roles. Those aspirations don't seem to us to be in conflict in an educational system that is not divided by antagonistic debate. The gifted and talented parents in the anti-Connected Math campaign (see Chapter 2) are a good example. They seem to us to want their children's individual talents nurtured, and they want them to have profound mathematical knowledge. Implicitly they want them trained for good careers (i.e., by getting high SAT scores, going to top schools, etc.) so that they will have access to positional goods. If we look at the claims Lisa Delpit (1995) makes for black youngsters, we will find the same kind of claim: what she rightly objects to is the notion that black children somehow can't be expected to have academic expectations. A coherent public education should, we think, draw on all three purposes.

The redundancy of the division of purposes

Our second thought is that the emergence of these three educational purposes was a feature of a historical context now passed, so now we really are just fighting old battles. This requires a lengthy explanation. What did the founders of the Republic believe about education? If you have visited the Thomas Jefferson memorial in Washington, DC, you will read the phrase "Establish the law for educating the common people. This it is the business of the state to effect and on a general plan." Jefferson's call for a system of public education was essential to the conception of being a citizen in a democracy. If people are going to be well informed, enough to make judgments, they would need to be able to understand at least some of the complex problems that crop up. Jefferson, like most of his contemporaries, believed strongly in individual rights, freedom of conscience, religion, and speech – the acknowledgement of the centrality of the individual in American life. Yet he also believed in "one nation under God," one in which individuals came together as democrats (i.e., for their society). For this they needed knowledge. Jefferson would have seen three aspects of one purpose, not three educational purposes in conflict. Americans needed an education that included specific information necessary for free people (knowledge) as democratic citizens (self), in order to contribute to society (society). Of course, upbringing and wealth would affect how people developed educational interests. As an aside, Jefferson did make a strong appeal for universal public education, and he was a Virginian. Virginia did not pass a law for universal public education until about 1890, while New England, and much of the North, had universal education from the mid 1600s.

If this is an accurate representation of the views of Thomas Jefferson and other Founding Fathers, how did this dramatic three-fold division of purpose arise? That's a complex historical question to which we can only give a rough answer here. The significant context for the development of the divisions was the exponential growth of the United States – from a population of around 5 million in 1800 to over 250 million people in 2000, from a rural vastness into an industrial, commercial, and military giant, and from a country dominated by an ethnic (white) majority into a more cosmopolitan society, especially when it began to put to rest in the twentieth century the evils of slavery and racism.

How did that affect views of educational purpose? In the late nineteenth and early twentieth centuries, as the country started to burst into its industrial complexity, there developed an intense struggle for the curriculum, for what/how children should learn (Kleibard, 1995). There were huge demands from industry and commerce for trained labor. Different views of scholarship emerged. Free Americans wanted, as Emerson's essay on *The American Scholar* suggests, a break with European traditions of knowledge and the creation of new understandings. The country was heavy with immigrants speaking many different languages. The United States needed its immigrants to be taught to be Americans. The tensions that resulted led to emphases on one segment of educational purpose against another.

Moreover, public education was not all sweetness and light. For a start, huge numbers of male teachers had died or been killed between 1860 and 1865. Massive increases in the numbers of children to be schooled presented woman-power problems for education. Ideals like Horace Mann's common school were developed, but the system was run by conservatives, as the influential philosopher John Dewey (1969) pointed out in 1904. The fierce independence of the free American living in her/his community also meant that schools were run as local rural enterprises through school boards (and they *still* have the schedules to match!). Educational expenditure – namely, taxes – was always a matter of local controversy. College and university education expanded out of all recognition, especially with the foundation of land-grant colleges. Before and during World War I, high schools started to offer more vocational and technical courses, with some advocates arguing that this should be their primary concern rather than the (often European) "knowledge" that elementary children were forced to learn by rote.

By the early 1900s, the romantic view of the little red schoolhouse on the prairie had atrophied into an elementary education where children's work was driven by rote learning from textbooks written by university professors (Rugg, 1926). Ideas for the kindergarten had been imported from Europe in the second half of the nineteenth century with the idea that the child was the center (Chung and Walsh, 2000). The individual was all important. Why was this attractive? Apart from the romantic philosophies driving this movement, the idea of the child's uniqueness fell on fertile American ground precisely because the child of the time was not being treated as an individual in rote-driven puni-tive schools. From the kindergarten, therefore, was launched an ideal of the individual child as the center of education which became labeled "progressive." Play was a child's work. When a person says "give them time to be children" today, s/he is talking progressive language.

John Dewey began writing about education at the turn of that century. Within his complex and wide-ranging views on education set out over half a century from 1900 to his death in 1952, Dewey believed that the child's inter-ests were of paramount importance, but that schools should also be nurseries of democracy where children learnt by doing, by engaging in social action. Indeed, Dewey was also an early advocate of trade schools because they offered children the opportunity to follow their interests. Dewey thus thought it important to integrate the three distinct educational purposes within a concept of the growth of the democratic free American, although his view of knowledge was pragmatic (and American as opposed to European) and anything but traditional. Nevertheless he had to write *Experience and Education* to disown those of his followers who thought there were no traditions of knowledge to inherit (Dewey, 1963).

What does this location of the issue of context suggest?

In a relatively simple democratic society, like that of the Union in 1800, people can articulate a general (and usually minimal) purpose for public educa-tion.

In a complex industrial society, as the institutions of public education develop, a traditional view of knowledge is challenged by industrial purposes because it lacks application. Social and vocational purposes rise in importance. In Victorian England, for example, the curriculum of the "public" (private) schools reflected the vocational interests of the rising middle class. In the United States, and parts of Europe, social and vocational purposes were opposed by the principle of personal freedom, which was seen as a right and a possession of the individual child. New pressures of growth and change break down the integrated educational purpose of a simple society, and those tensions become magnified.

Yet times have drastically changed. No longer do industrial purposes call for a labor force sweating at the doors of blast furnaces, or, for that matter, children doing their own thing oblivious of social needs. A complex post-industrial tech-nological society, such as ours, needs creative, enlightened, educated people confident as individuals but cognizant of the needs of our complex society and, of course, able to use computers and related machines for human purposes. The division of the three purposes was relevant to an age and a context. Each has general validity and importance for our present context. The challenge is to get on with finding ways to integrate and reconcile them.

Let's review the first two thoughts described in this chapter. Our first thought was that it is possible for the three educational purposes to be integrated and complementary. Our second thought was that the emergence of these three educational purposes was a feature of a historical context now passed. Perhaps neither are correct. They are intended to help you locate the issues from a reconciliatory stance as you create your own discussions.

Our third thought reveals similarities and differences between the three positions.

Teaching children to value

At the heart of the conflict between the three educational purposes is a conflict of value. It runs like this. Should children, in general, learn things like literature, art, music, and history that are deemed to be worthwhile just for themselves? Or, should their (present) values be developed so that they are accustomed to choice as they grow up? Or, should they learn skills, trades, or accomplishments that have a cash value as they enter the marketplace?

Let us approach these questions in this way. Imagine a baseball fan. The fan watches every game, reads the sports columns avidly, goes to matches when s/he can, takes the spouse and children along, supported by evening excitements in the yard where the children become baseball players like Cal Ripken, Mark McGwire, or Sammy Sosa. If we ask this fan why s/he does all this, what kind of answers do we get?

The fan will talk about the tradition of the game in the United States.

The fan will talk of her/his own family tradition – "my dad always took me and his dad took him."

The fan will talk about the game itself – "I love the game, it's fun, it's exciting." OK, we say, but what is it (you value) about this game?

Oh, it's the traditional challenge of teams (Yankees versus Orioles). The game also brings out players' personalities, their courage, skill, speed, and strength, the team as a team. It can also be very dramatic, s/he will tell us.

Notice that our fan can give us answers to our question about why s/he values baseball by first locating her/himself historically (the traditions) and then describing the features of the game and the contest.

But if we now say to the fan, "OK, we see all that, but what *use* is baseball to you?" or "What do you watch baseball *for*?" the short answer will probably be something like "Hey, it's not the sort of thing that can be of use, you know, like cash in the bank, or a hammer, or a plane trip." For this fan watching baseball is not supposed to be of *use* as if it were a tool to get somewhere else, to get a better job, to get rich. Baseball has value for the fan and the family internal or intrinsic to itself. So the fan doesn't watch baseball *in order to* have a good time:

watching baseball *is* having a good time. Baseball has no value beyond itself, no external or instrumental value. That's not true for everyone, of course. Every time the fan goes to the game s/he buys a hotdog from the guy running his stand. This guy hates the game, thinks it boring and a waste of time, but he values baseball for its extrinsic value: he makes money out of it.

And as the baseball fan feels about baseball, so poets feel about poetry, philosophers about philosophy, scientists about science, computer buffs about computers, mathematicians about mathematics, musicians about music, and lovers of literature about novels. They value these things for their own sake. It is this kind of internal or intrinsic value that those who advocate a curriculum based on "the life of the mind" want children to have, and their teachers too.

Contrast our baseball fan now with a person who always sees the world in instrumental, external, or extrinsic terms. S/he is the sort of person who always needs a carrot to "come on board" for any enterprise. S/he is the person who is always asking "What's in it for me?" Some men and women look on marriage like this. Their choice of a partner is not determined so much by love of their mate, but what s/he can get out of it! They see marriage as something that gets them status, or free sex, and free meals. Having children is good, not for the love or companionship, but because they will be praised for their achievements. If you teach them right, they'll care for you in your old age, or "why else would you have children?"

Yet there is a profound paradox about American society. On the one hand, people prize material things very highly. They are driven by the achievement motive. They want to get these positional goods, they want power, wealth, their version of the American Dream. On the other hand, many Americans are fascinated by their hobbies, their pets, their passions, and their commitments that have no "use." Most people do understand this paradox about what they value: they know the difference between loving someone for themselves and their faults and loving someone for what they can get out of them. They love their dog not just because it is of use as a guard dog, but because it's a friendly companion. As they look at material goods, they do ask: "Yes, but what do I want it *for?*" As people like Jay Gatsby find, merely pursuing wealth becomes ultimately pointless: What do you do with it? What is it *for?*

How children come to value things is another way to examine the conflict between the three educational purposes. Should children, in general, learn things that are regarded, like literature, art, music, and history, as of intrinsic or internal value, as worthwhile in themselves? Should children learn skills that have instrumental or extrinsic value, that have a cash value as they enter the marketplace? Each purpose contains a concept of value that it is critical for children to acquire.

How, then, can children be taught, or acquire, a sense of value?

Here are four initial possible similarities between the three purposes. Children should:

- Come to value what they learn in schools.
- Understand intrinsic value. That is, they should learn about baseball, or citizenship, or their own painting for the activity itself.
- Learn what extrinsic value is. That is, they should understand what it is to value things for their usefulness as instruments to get them someplace else.
- Come to know the difference between doing something for the enjoyment and doing something for some instrumental end.

But, we need to ask, as children learn things, do they get a sense of value? And if they get some sense of value for certain things, what is the reason they come to value these particular things? For each person, in principle, is always able to choose what s/he does, whatever the obstacles put in the way. When we make choices, we are making a statement about what we value. Since the freedom to choose is central to democratic life, and since children don't come into the world endowed with that capacity, in the course of a child's education, s/he must get taught a sense of value.

However, there is one further crucial similarity directly connected to the conflict of purposes:

- Children and students get very confused about value – whichever educational purpose governs their work.

Let's explain. Our purpose here is not to be critical, but to give what we see as a factual account. Sometimes children are told about the value of what they are learning as intrinsic, which can also sound very high-minded. Learning this is Fun! Exciting! Valuable! Crucial to your life as a person! The child may not be convinced: "Why do we have to do quadratic equations," the child asks, "if we are never going to use them?" "Well, they're very interesting." "Oh yeah?" But much of the time children also get the extrinsic justification for what they are learning. "You need to learn this if you're going to college," "you need to pass this test or the school will be shut down," "you have to learn this stuff to graduate," or "your parents will be disappointed." Parents sometimes pay children for getting good grades, so children pester teachers for better grades not because they care about the quality of their work, but because they want money from their parents. Schooling seems to be riddled with instrumental purpose and value. Indeed, even those who regard education as of intrinsic value often cop out by motivating children through the lure of what economists call positional goods, that is the wealth or resources (the goods) which determine a person's position in society. Long before a child is out of elementary school, therefore, s/he understands perfectly well that what s/he learns at school has cash value. A person "needs" certificates, awards, grades, credits to get into the "right" college or university, get a better job, house, cars, salaries. Schooling determines our qualifications in the labor market. Children imbibe this knowledge with their mother's milk. Or at least, many do. For those that do not, they eventually drop out of school; for whatever reason, these children have suffered from not being taught anything that would have helped them to develop a sense of value.

Those who value knowledge as the educational purpose and those who emphasize the individual usually deploy some intrinsic statements about value. Those advocating a social purpose are more likely to speak of extrinsic value. The brute fact is that the messages are confused throughout schooling and university education. If education were driven by a coherent unified purpose, people would pay better attention to developing in children and understanding both types of value. Both would be emphasized because both are important if our account of a complex technological society is accurate.

But here's a final similarity among these general purposes:

- Everyone wants children to be motivated to learn.

How do we get children motivated? Behind all the hooks and gimmicks, the strategies and tactics, the psychology and the sociology, we have only two basic ways. We either get them interested (the intrinsic value) or provide a carrot or a stick (the extrinsic value). (Recall the agreement on extrinsic motivation among the math educators.) At the end of the day, all issues of motivation are issues about the ways we want children to value what they do.

The little matter of poetry

In what seems a purely intrinsic value matter, the extrinsic creeps in. Poetry enthusiasts are, as we said, like the baseball fan. When we ask them why they value it, they may tell us a story about their past, but they can only describe its features to us. So they will want children to read the psalms for their emotional and spiritual power, Shakespeare's sonnets for their erotic content, Longfellow's poetry for its rhythms and the purity of its American sensitivity. If they are traditionalists, they will create a curriculum that probably excludes children writing their own poetry. If they are committed to the individual purpose, they will want children to begin to write it, and they might start with the rhymes and natural rhythms of rap or hip-hop, or the blues. They believe that children should encounter poetry, let us say, because it can enrich their lives, give them vehicles for their emotions, and depth in their expression. And they start, not with *Ode to a Nightingale*, but where the children are. Yet both purposes imply that to write or speak poetically is to have a particular kind of voice in the conversation of humankind (Oakeshott, 1967). Just as you have to develop your voice to sing in a choir, so you will develop your poetic voice by listening, reading, and writing.

So, on this explanation of the intrinsic value of poetry as something to be known and experienced, both the traditionalist and the progressive are committed. The latter sees children being encouraged to write and experience poetry, their own and their friends', as well as the poetry expressed in plays and drama. They are encouraged to construct meaning, but, of course, they can't do this without encountering some content, and they will probably experience some "great" literature, albeit not in the dimensions that one would expect of the traditionalist, where a semester's work may be defined under such a heading as "The Metaphysical Poets." At the level of general purpose, the progressive is not suggesting that there is nothing of value to be learned or experienced in the work of other people, alive or dead. S/he just places more attention on what children do rather than on what they read of others. As far as the content is concerned, a child from a traditional or a progressive school will probably know Shakespeare and Longfellow (or whoever). So from two purposes, advocates want children to enjoy this form of human expression for its own sake.

But could poetry be of instrumental value? Well, it can get results. Whisper your lover one of Elizabeth Barrett Browning's *Sonnets from the Portuguese* – "How do I love thee? Let me count the ways" – and see what happens! Patriotic songs started their life as verse and national anthems are not noted for the quality of their meter, but for the patriotism they embody and produce in citizens. An aggressive and interesting argument about what "children need to know" comes from E. D. Hirsch Jr., who believes that Americans are culturally illiterate, that this is a relatively recent development, and the fault of progressive education, which, he claims, has ruined the system. Be that as it may, Hirsch's (1996) view of what children need to know starts out by being entirely traditional. He has rounded up all the usual suspects in terms of subjects – history, science, English, math, geography. Yet Hirsch never really says that these things are good because they are interesting, because they are valuable in themselves. He argues that you need them for some other extrinsic end. You need to be socialized: you need to know a lot of "stuff," as Pam calls it, to be a member of society. For Hirsch, poetry appears to be valuable only for its *instrumental, not its intrinsic value*. If he did see it as having primarily intrinsic value, he would pay much more attention to the notion of how children come to value it, and how it could be connected to different motivations children have and the contexts in which they are placed.

What the little matter of poetry tells us is that there is no clear-cut division between intrinsic and extrinsic value. To build an educational system on one or the other seems to neglect the importance of children understanding and experiencing both. For there is a continuum running, say, from the pure love for another person (at the intrinsic end) to the usefulness of a nail (at the extrinsic end). There is therefore all the more reason for children to become sophisticated in their sense of value. Victorian Englishmen were taught Latin both for its own sake and because it was thought to develop qualities of mind useful in running an empire. Published poets love writing poetry and they make money from it. Few of them, if any, do it just for the money. Indeed, most poets probably would not stop writing even if they made no money from it at all. There is an intrinsic and an instrumental side to most everything we learn. After all, it's quite useful to quote Shakespeare in our e-mail.

So, our third thought runs like this. Offering children, like Jack and Garrett, educational activities driven by all of the three educational purposes will enable them to test out different kinds of motivation and to deepen their understanding of what it is to value things. This sense of value, connected as it is to what people choose, is at the heart of the personal freedoms treasured in a democratic society. Our sense of value is on a continuum from the purely intrinsic to the simply extrinsic or instrumental. Maybe we are confusing children about value because we can't reconcile educational purposes. One possible outcome of RD would be for educational practice to develop a more coherent sense of teaching children ways in which to place value on their activities, aspirations, and ambitions.

10 Conclusion
The need for RD

Integrating the three educational purposes, teaching children about value, and adopting a reconciliatory stance in conversation present difficult challenges. We should not, however, be discouraged or dissuaded by the difficulty and the apparent idealistic nature of the process of reconciliation. We believe change can happen and the first step is for people to simply start thinking about educational controversy differently. We need to recognize the impact of the argument culture (Tannen, 1998) on our lives and whether it is inevitable in the type of society we want to develop and nurture.

We started this book by talking about differences in Hugh and Pamela's experiences. Our experience of writing this book and using RD is that once people start thinking about conversation differently, they begin to hear things they never noticed before. People seem to argue much of the time, constantly criticize each other, work to poke holes in each other's theories, complain and vent, rather than seek appropriate dialogue that could help them solve their problems. Don't misconstrue our intentions, however. In advocating RD, we are not saying that people should never state an opinion or provide constructive criticism or that we should avoid the critical altogether. We believe people who care for us the most, and trust us completely, are those who provide straightforward, honest feedback and criticism. But, most of the time, when it is truly appropriate for people to provide criticism, people are either antagonistic or they turn their backs, afraid to be honest. So there are four reasons why RD is important and these involve the political, moral, civic, and social needs of our society.

The political need

One reason why antagonistic debate in education has become so demoralizing is that division and dissension about the purposes of the school enable any and every side to make the school a scapegoat. That deflects attention from the divisive political debates, special interests, etc., which actually foster the conflict. Antagonistic debate enables those outside the schools to put the blame on them.

To be fair, we need to recognize the school's achievements. During the 1990s the economy in the United States has become a bounding colossus with productivity and output outpacing every other industrialized nation. But often these successes are not attributed to the school. The American teachers' contribution to this dynamism needs to be recognized and appreciated (Berliner, 1995). They carry a (major) share of the responsibility for the character, creativity, and ingenuity of the American workforce.

To be just, we have to validate people's efforts. There are countless dedicated teachers and administrators, struggling productively and humanely with immense problems under extremely difficult conditions.

To be responsible, we need to admit that teachers (alone) cannot be held to account for pervasive social changes. They continue their dedication even though there have been drastic changes in social life (Elkind, 1994). If we stop blaming the schools, then we will be moving away from an antagonistic style. RD can therefore:

- bring about a more productive political environment for education in which the schools are not singled out as objects for attack;
- celebrate the fact that every citizen shares in the mutual responsibility for education; and thereby
- enable everyone to exercise their civic rights more thoroughly.

The moral need

One morally objectionable outcome of antagonistic public debate is that most citizens, parents, and teachers get shut out of the debate. The forensic, silver, or sharp-tongued quickness of the professional politician, academic, journalist, or entertainer is not a quality most people have. Most of us can hold conversations, even if we get irritable within them. Most of us can take time to think through problems with those close to us, but we are not in business as, or trained to be, slick speakers or debaters. Constantly faced with these examples, we assume that antagonism and confrontation is the only strategy to get anywhere. Antagonism makes us all create protective barriers. Otherwise we switch off. Antagonistic discourse marginalizes the ordinary person and the average citizen.

RD can therefore:

- enable us to initiate a conversation, whether we feel on the top or the bottom – we can be a participant, not a spectator;
- provide a public space for us where the conversation aims at reconciliation, not conflict; and
- provide easy and legitimate ways for people to enter this new kind of conversation.

The civic need

One of the complexities in democratic societies lies in the commitment to personal freedom. Among many other things this means that everyone has the right, whether they exercise it or not, to contribute to deciding what should be done in the future. Yet the United States is also a land of immigrants. The public forum is full of differing ideals and ideas for discussion. This is a matter for pride and joy, not for despair. It applies at the interpersonal level. As authors, we have grown tremendously from our interactions with each other. We "come from" different places, to be sure, so we think about things differently. Hugh is a recent immigrant from Britain. Pamela considers herself a Californian, regardless of where she was born or where she is presently living. But we are able to listen to each other and build upon those differences, rather than getting embroiled in unsolvable arguments and being worried about our egos. Our sense of ourselves as people and as citizens carries with it openness to rational argument.

As we finish this book, we recognize that there are serious, even ferocious, culture wars in progress in the country (Hunter, 1994). American social mores are not merely diverse. They are under major assault from such conservative writers as Robert Bork (2000) and Bill Bennett (1998). Robert Hughes's caustic *Culture of Complaint* (1993) makes the direct comparison between the contemporary United States and the Roman Empire in its last days. Such angry texts concentrate on ideas that divide rather than unite us. In some ways, that is one of the hidden consequences of democratic success and of peacetime. Free from external pressure, we go back to an emphasis on differences. But, while free speech and dissent are the life-blood of a democracy, they have to be the prelude to agreement and to building on the best, classically illustrated in the history of the foundation of the Republic.

We believe it will be more productive to listen and to compromise, to seek out the best in the different views portrayed. Common purpose is as important to the democratic citizen as are her/his individual rights, to free speech, and so on.
RD can:

- provide for the development of civic trust through determining a mutual goal; and
- provide a civic process for examining both previous solutions and alternative descriptions of problems.

We believe it is a basis for a long-lasting treaty in the ever-threatening culture wars.

The social need

We have noted the need to expect longer horizons for improvement, especially in education. This reminds us of a *Star Trek Next Generation* episode. In that episode, two alien races had been at war for many years. The starship *Enterprise* was ordered to assist an ambassador in his mission to bring these two enemies together. During the first meeting, hostilities broke out and people were killed. The ambassador was left without a translator to help him communicate with these aliens. Both sides lost trust. They blamed each other for this mishap and for other transgressions. Both groups were very angry. The ambassador was ready to give up, but the captain of the starship convinced him to forge on. By the end, the aliens who were involved in the negotiations agreed to work together to learn each other's language and also the ambassador's language before starting the negotiations. At one point someone said, "But that will take a very long time." And the ambassador said, "Yes and that is exactly what we need." They needed time to get to know each other and learn about each other before negotiations could begin; they needed to build trust.

The long haul is the only viable route to the improvement of public education, even though that clashes so violently with political timetables and elections and social expectations. Our individual children are not in school very long, so we need to be conscious of our civic responsibilities before we worry about the education of our grandchildren! Socially we need a discourse that demands balance, patience, commitment, mutual respect, extreme care, and the virtues foreign to antagonistic public debate.

Taking this route is not to suggest that education can be taken out of civic politics: that's impossible in a democratic society. Every institution can be improved. But taking the long haul seriously demands a new kind of debate in which winning is not the objective. The task is to build on the best.

RD can therefore:

- foster all the civic virtues;
- gradually change social expectations through understanding complexity; and
- implicitly support goals which are steps to continuous improvement, not the proven achievements of a controlling position.

The ideas presented in this book are not hopelessly idealistic. We are constantly being told by teachers who work with us that reframing their professional commitments under the context of moral professionalism (Sockett, 1993) has been exceedingly helpful to them in their work (Sockett *et al.*, 2001). They tell us stories about their success with other teachers, with administrators, and with parents as they move away from antagonistic argument and adopt the role as the one caring (Noddings, 1984, Chapter 2) who strives to create partnerships (how can we work together to accomplish our goals?). If we change the way we approach others, people do respond differently. We need to make this "non-traditional approach" the norm.

In this book, we have worked to accomplish three goals: (a) convince people to change their orientation toward educational controversy from antagonistic to moral, (b) work to define problems, and (c) open up new possibilities for alternative solutions. After naming and analyzing some of the difficulties we face in education, it is clear that we need to do things differently. We believe we must make a start with the character of our dialogue, even if it is only in terms of the moral and intellectual habits we bring to debates in our families and in our workplaces.

Appendix

A protocol for reconciliatory discourse

This protocol is intended for use by groups of people with differing points of view on educational matters to find ways to reconcile their views through the careful articulation of a mutually agreed problem to which they can then seek a solution for their context. Unless otherwise stated, tasks are for the group of participants.

The reconciliatory discourse (RD) procedure is therefore intended for use in a formal context. As has been consistently emphasized, this will take time. A group should therefore plan its time realistically. We envision this protocol, if followed carefully, to take at least eight 2–3 hour sessions. We advise either a regular weekly meeting or a meeting over a day and a half to two days.

1   Establishing responsibilities

    1.1   Give brief bio-statements and commitments.
    1.2   Selection of a Chairperson (see article 8).
    1.3   Selection of Recorder (see article 9).
    1.4   Determine a time frame for initial discussion (see above).
    1.5   Read the description of RD:

> RD is a civil discussion in which participants with divergent views seek to build common ground for (educational) practice through the articulation of a shared problem to which they are all morally and intellectually committed. Participants in RD use compromise, adopt middle ways, and make practical choices to build on the best. They respect divergence and eschew consensus for consensus' sake. They use its principles in writing as well as in practice-oriented discourse. Their purpose is to make better public and private judgments about education.

    1.6   Discuss and accept the following responsibilities:
        (a)   Acknowledge the authority of the chair.
        (b)   Be open to moral and ideological reconciliation.
        (c)   Commitment to uphold the Constitution and the rule of law.
        (d)   Respect for where people are coming from.
        (e)   Accept responsibility for the fairness of a discussion and opportunities for all participants.

(f) Seek self- and group improvement in the disciplines of discourse, namely: listening, expressing oneself effectively, personal interaction, and searching and learning through deliberation.

2 The procedure

2.1 Discuss outline task within the RD procedure.

Note: "it is important to name the problem precisely because all the work to follow will be directed at correcting the problem as it has been named" (Kepner and Tregoe, 1997, p. 29).

    I   Locate the issues
    II   Work out similarities and differences
    III Rank similarities in order of importance
    IV Establish inter-relationships
    V   Formulate the shared problem

2.2 Recorder to note problems and ambiguities and establish group agreement to the list.

3 Locate the issues

3.1 Describe the oppositions and their origins.
    3.1.1 The Chair initiates topic for discussion.
    3.1.2 Q: Is the topic description roughly right?
    3.1.3 Q: What are the general positions represented here? Participants outline a position in turn until all are identified with one.
    3.1.4 Context Q: What's the present context for this problem? Historical Q: How, in brief, did it get this way?
    3.1.5 Recorder summarizes.

3.2 Identify any hidden issues.
    3.2.1 Chair describes a "hidden" issue.
    3.2.2 Q: Do participants have sensitive issues they won't discuss?

3.3 Identify any surrogate problems.
    3.3.1 Chair defines a surrogate issue.
    3.3.2 Q: Is the topic so far described the topic participants really want to discuss?

3.4 Product 1: Recorder summarizes description of oppositions, preferably with a document to be agreed.

4 Work out similarities and differences

4.1 Revisit the conditions and requirements for participants.
    4.1.1 Evaluate whether conditions are being met (1.6(a)–(c)).
    4.1.2 Evaluate whether the requirements are being met (1.6(d)–(f)).

4.1.3   Chair does short summary of evaluation comments.

4.2   Suspend judgment.
    4.2.1   Chair and Recorder provide examples of failures to search for understanding from the discussion.
    4.2.2   Discuss and outline strategies for this search, for example "Do I understand what is being said?" and "getting distance."
    4.2.3   Discussion of Chair's responsibility to call breaches of suspension of judgment.

4.3   Describe self-interests and participant power relations.
    4.3.1   Extended bio-statement of self-interests versus others and the topic.
    4.3.2   All describe power relations internal and external to the group.
    4.3.3   Does evaluation (4.1.1 and 4.1.2) reveal power relations?

4.4   Set out central values and outcomes.
    4.4.1   Prepare individual written position/value statements for circulation.
    4.4.2   State value positions briefly and concisely (see models in text, pp. 29–30, 46).
    4.4.3   Individuals to read out loud and explain value positions other than their own.
    4.4.4   Mutual check for understanding of divergent views.
    4.4.5   Construct list of practical outcomes from value positions relevant to topic.

4.5   Identify perceived similarities and differences.
    4.5.1   Prepare individual written description of similarities without searching for consensus.
    4.5.2   Revisit the topic and redescribe it.
    4.5.3   Individuals to exchange and read aloud similarities as seen by others.
    4.5.4   Individuals and group to list differences.
    4.5.5   Decision point if few similarities: see article 10.

4.6   Recorder to outline Product 2: The initial agenda of similarities and differences.

5   Rank similarities in order of importance

5.1   Examine the progress of the discourse.
    5.1.1   Revisit earlier evaluation (4.1).
    5.1.2   Evaluate the sense of trust and collaboration in the group.
    5.1.3   Identify the areas of intellectual struggle.
    5.1.4   Recorder will list items of moral and intellectual significance.

5.2   Work out those differences on which agreement is unlikely.
    5.2.1   Individuals produce written lists.
    5.2.2   Discuss composite list to which all must assent.

5.3   Isolate the differences in which few have an investment and set aside.
    5.3.1   Individuals produce written list.
    5.3.2   Discuss composite list to check that the items should not be either in 5.2, or revisited as possible similarities.

5.4   Rank the similarities in order of importance (see article 11).
    5.4.1   Revisit similarities.
    5.4.2   Individuals produce written rankings.
    5.4.3   Discuss results.
    5.4.4   Individuals revisit rankings.
    5.4.5   Group examines common rankings.

5.5   Recorder to outline Product 3: The agenda of differences and similarities.

6   Establish inter-relationships

6.1   Establish common educational practices from the list of similarities.
    6.1.1   Review the common ground from polarized positions.
    6.1.2   Individuals present evidence of practice derived from similarities.
    6.1.3   Examine and identify inter-relationships between practices.

6.2   Define mutual interdependencies of similar practices.
    6.2.1   Identify formerly polarized positions to describe the character of the reconciliation: "reconciliation can be a matter of compromise, of taking a centrist view, or of integrating positions to establish common ground."
    6.2.2   Identify practices which are mutually interdependent.

6.3   Recorder to develop list of practical relationships and interdependencies.

7   Formulate the shared problem

7.1   Define the problem
    7.1.1   Review each product:
        (a)   description of oppositions,
        (b)   initial agenda, and
        (c)   developed agenda of differences and similarities.
    7.1.2   Individuals to write down the problem perceived:
        State the problem as a question.
        Keep the question short.
        Never state the question as an either–or.

       7.1.3   Circulate copies of individuals' statements.

       7.1.4   Define the problem.

7.2   Develop a plan of action.

       7.2.1   Move toward a solution to the problem? Or, re-examine the steps? Or, terminate the conversation?

       7.2.2   Conduct situational analysis with view to solving problem.

       7.2.3   Develop action agenda.

7.3   Product: Full statement of the problem with an agreed agenda for action.

7.4   Learning (evaluation: see article 13)

8   The role of the Chair

The primary task of the Chair is to be responsible for the organization and conduct of meetings. The Chair must:

(a)   Have a working knowledge of the principles and goals of RD.

(b)   Be strictly impartial between oppositions, regarding the reconciliation of positions held by *these participants* as the goal.

(c)   Seek to protect divergent views, for reconciliation does not mean consensus.

(d)   Exercise imagination in asking questions or framing oppositions differently.

(e)   Insist on the group focusing on specific questions.

The Chair should use the protocol as the usual guide, but, depending on the character of the group, it may not need to be used slavishly.

The Chair should invite the group to audio-record the meeting and the tape should be a source of learning for the Chair.

9   The role of the Recorder

The Recorder should *not* be a participant.

The primary task of the Recorder is to document the main conclusions of the group's discussions. These occur at the following points:

2.2   Problems and ambiguities arising from discussion of the outline.

3.4   Initial description of oppositions. Initial agenda of similarities and differences.

5.5   The final agenda of similarities and differences (with rankings).

6.3   The list of common educational practices.

7.3   The defined problem.

Written copies of each of these should be available and the Recorder should also file copies of individuals' statements.

The Recorder should, wherever possible, provide a cumulative copy of the documents to all participants.

10 Should we continue? (4.5.5)

This is the context when the group has a large list of differences and few similarities.

The Chair should summarize the differences after the group's acknowledgement that it has not developed a sufficient base of similarities to make further discussion obviously profitable.

We strongly advise the Chair to break the discussion (i.e., for 20 minutes, or overnight depending on the context) to allow participants to reflect.

The Chair should seek to keep the focus on the character of the differences, not on, say, individual impatience or personality dissonance.

The Chair should not seek, however, to keep discussion going for the sake of it and we recommend a voting process taken in the following order:

(1) To end the discussion. If this vote is lost, then
(2) to break now for a defined period (week/overnight). If this vote is lost, then
(3) to have the group work out its schedule for the future and where it wishes to re-engage in the agenda.

11 The ranking process

This is a simple process. Given a list of similarities by the Recorder, each person puts a number against each with 1 being the most important to that person. The Recorder then adds the numbers from all participants for each similarity. The group order of importance of the similarities will then be from the lowest to the highest number. However, it should be noted that where there is a substantial gap, those similarities numerically below the gap will have the greatest support.

12 Learning evaluation

Participants should be asked the following questions:

1 Did you feel to have built a basis of trust with other participants?

2 Was the declaration of self-interest and power relationships significant in this building, and if so, why?

3 Have you developed personal, moral, and intellectual skills in general during this RD? Has it helped you to
(a) suspend judgment,
(b) get inside the views of an opponent,

      (c)   attend closely evidence,

      (d)   make decisions on the basis of importance?

4   Have you developed your skills in the disciplines of discourse?

      (a)   Listening

      (b)   Self-expression

      (c)   Personal interaction

      (d)   Searching and learning through deliberation.

5   What are the difficulties and problems you see in RD which arise from this experience of it?

6   Will you use the procedure in other contexts?

Bibliography

Adler, M., Petch, A., and Tweedie, J. (1989). *Parental Choice and Education Policy*. Edinburgh: Edinburgh University Press.

Airasian, P. W. (1997). *Classroom Assessment*, Third Edition. New York: McGraw-Hill.

Almarode, M., Cordray-Van de Castle, K., Hanrahan, M., and Rossell, S. (2000). "Assessment Through Portfolio Exhibition." Unpublished research report, Initiatives in Education Transformation, George Mason University.

Banks, O. (1986). *Becoming a Feminist: The Social Origins of 'First Wave' Feminism*. Athens, GA: University of Georgia Press.

Baron, M. A. and Boschee, F. (1995). *Authentic Assessment: The Key to Unlocking Student Success*. Lancaster, PA: Technomic.

Barrett, D. (1997). *The Paradox Process. Creative Business Solutions ... Where You Least Expect to Find Them*. New York: Amacom, American Management Association.

Belenky, M. F., Clinchy, B. M., Goldberger, N. R., and Tarule, J. M. (1986). *Women's Ways of Knowing*. New York: Basic Books.

Bennett, W. (1998). *The Death of Outrage: Bill Clinton and the Assault on American Ideals*. New York: Free Press.

Benning, V. (1999). "Doubts Arise on Low Scores: Parents, Officials Fear Tests Flawed." *Washington Post*, January 14.

Berliner, D. C. (1995). *The Manufactured Crisis: Myths, Fraud, and the Attack on America's Public Schools*. Reading, MA: Addison-Wesley.

Bork, R. (2000). *Slouching towards Gomorrah*. New York: HarperCollins.

Boswell, T. (1999). "Sometimes Winning Can Be a Losing Cause." *Washington Post*, November 28.

Bowe, R., Ball, S. J., and Gold, A. (1992). *Reforming Education and Changing Schools: Case Studies in Policy Sociology*, London and New York: Routledge.

Boyer, E. (1983). *High School*. New York: Harper and Row.

Boyer, E. (1990). *Scholarship Reconsidered: Priorities of the Professoriate*. New York: Carnegie Foundation for the Advancement of Teaching.

Bracey, G. W. (1994). "The Fourth Bracey Report on the Condition of Public Education." *Phi Delta Kappa*, October, 115–116.

Brighouse, H. (2000). *School Choice and Social Justice*. Oxford: Oxford University Press.

Carnegie Foundation for the Advancement of Teaching (1992). *School Choice*. Princeton, NJ: Carnegie Foundation.

Chubb, J. E. and Moe, T. M. (1990). *Politics, Markets, and America's Schools*. Washington, DC: Brookings Institution.

Chung, S. and Walsh, D. (2000). "Unpacking Child Centeredness: A History of Meanings." *Journal of Curriculum Studies*, 32(2), 215–235.

Cibulka, J. (1990). "Choice and Restructuring American Education." In W. L. Boyd and H. J. Walberg, *Choice in Education: Potential and Problems*. Berkeley, CA: McCutchan.

Cohen, E. G. (1994). *Designing Groupwork*. New York: Teachers College Press.

Collingwood, R. G. (1946). *The Idea of History*. New York: Oxford University Press.

Darling-Hammond, L. (1997). "Reforming the School Reform Agenda: Developing Capacity for School Transformation." In E. Clinchy (ed.), *Transforming Public Education*. New York: Teachers College Press.

Darling-Hammond, L., Ancess, J., and Falk, B. (1995). *Authentic Assessment in Action*. New York: Teachers College Press.

Delpit, L. (1995). *Other People's Children: Cultural Conflict in the Classroom*. New York: The New Press.

Dewey, J. (1963). *Experience and Education*. New York: Collier Macmillan.

Dewey, J. (1969 [1904]). *The Educational Situation*. New York: Arno Press and the New York Times.

Ebel, R. L. and Frisbie, D. A. (1991). *Essentials of Educational Measurement*. Englewood Cliffs, NJ: Prentice Hall.

Egan, K. (1997). *The Educated Mind*. Chicago: University of Chicago Press.

Elkind, D. (1994). *Ties That Stress*. Cambridge, MA: Harvard University Press.

Engel, M. (2000). *The Struggle for Control of Public Education: Market Ideology vs. Democratic Values*. Philadelphia, PA: Temple University Press.

Etzioni, A. (1996). *The New Golden Rule and Morality in a Democratic Society*. New York: Basic Books.

Fallows, J. (1997). *Breaking the News: How the Media Undermines American Democracy*. New York: Random House.

Finn, C. (1991). *We Must Take Charge!*. New York: Free Press.

Fliegel, S. and MacGuire, J. (1993). *Miracle in East Harlem: The Fight for Choice in Public Education*. New York: Times Books.

Franklin, Nancy (1999). "Not Entirely Clueless: New Shows about Teenagers." *New Yorker*, October 18 and 25, p. 232.

Gellman, E. S. (1995). *School Testing: What Parents and Educators Need to Know*. Westport, CT: Praeger.

Goodlad, J. I. (1994). *A Place Called School. Prospects for the Future*. New York: McGraw-Hill.

Goodman, W. (1998). "Unfazed by Excess, the Pundits Chatter On … and On." *New York Times*, December 9.

Grissmer, D. (1999). "Class Size Effects: Assessing the Evidence, Its Policy Implications, and Future Research Agenda." *Educational Evaluation & Policy Analysis*, 21(2), 231–248.

Guttman, A. and Thompson, D. (1996). *Democracy and Disagreement*. Cambridge, MA: Harvard University Press.

Habermas, J. (1994). "Further Reflections on the Public Sphere." In C. Calhoun (ed.), *Habermas and the Public Sphere*. Cambridge, MA: MIT Press.

Habermas, J. (1996). *Between Facts and Norms: Contributions to a Discourse Theory of Law and Democracy*. Cambridge, MA: MIT Press.

Haldane, J. B. S. (1947). "Organic Evolution." In *Encyclopedia Britannica, Volume 8*. Chicago: Encyclopedia Britannica.

Hanus, J. J. and Cookson, P. W. (1996). *Choosing Schools. Vouchers and American Education*. Washington, DC: American University Press.

Harding, S. (1991). *Whose Science? Whose Knowledge? Thinking from Women's Lives*. Ithaca, NY: Cornell University Press.

Henig, J. R. (1994). *Rethinking School Choice*. Princeton, NJ: Princeton University Press.

Hersch, P. (1998). *A Tribe Apart: A Journey into the Heart of American Adolescence*. New York: Fawcett Columbine.

Hirsch, E. D. (1996). *The Schools We Need and Why We Don't Have Them*. New York: Doubleday.

Hughes, R. (1993). *Culture of Complaint: The Fraying of America*. Oxford: Oxford University Press with New York: New York Public Library.

Hunter, J. (1994). *Before the Shooting Begins: The Struggle for Democracy in America's Culture Wars*. New York: Free Press.

Johnson, D. W. and Johnson, R. (1989). *Cooperation and Competition: Theory and Research*. Edina, MN: Interaction.

Johnson, D. W. and Johnson, R. (1994). *Learning Together and Alone. Cooperative, Competitive, and Individualistic Learning*. New York: Allyn and Bacon.

Kellaghan, T., Madaus, G. F., and Airasian, P. W. (1982). *The Effects of Standardized Testing*. Hingham, MA: Kluwer-Nijhoff.

Kepner, C. H. and Tregoe, B. B. (1997). *The New Rational Manager*. Princeton, NJ: Princeton Research Press.

Kleibard, H. M. (1995). *The Struggle for the American Curriculum 1893–1958*, Second Edition. New York: Routledge.

Kozol, J. (1991). *Savage Inequalities*. New York: Crown.

LePage-Lees, P. (1997). *From Disadvantaged Girls to Successful Women: Education and Women's Resiliency*. Westport, CT: Praeger.

Levine, L. W. (1990). *Highbrow–Lowbrow: The Emergence of Cultural Hierarchy in America*, William E. Massey, Sr. Lectures in the H Series 1986. Harvard, MA: Harvard University Press, September.

Lipset, S. M. (1996). *American Exceptionalism: A Double-edged Sword*. New York: W. W. Norton.

Mathews, J. (2000). "Connecticut's Education Success Story." *Washington Post*, July 18, p. A.11.

McMillan, J. H. (2001). *Essential Assessment Concepts for Teachers and Administrators*. Thousand Oaks, CA: Corwin Press.

Meier, D. (1995). *The Power of their Ideas*. Boston, MA: Beacon Press.

Meier, K. J. and Smith, K. B. (1995). *The Case Against School Choice: Politics, Markets & Fools*, New York: M. E. Sharpe.

Mills, J. (1996). *Partnership in the Primary School*. New York: Routledge.

Mitchell, R. (1992). *Testing for Learning: How New Approaches to Evaluation Can Improve American Schools*. New York: Free Press, Macmillan.

Morken, H. and Formicola, J. R. (1999). *The Politics of School Choice*. New York: Rowman & Littlefield.

Morse, J. (2001). "Do Charter Schools Pass the Test?" *Time*, 4 June, 157 (22), Time Inc.

National Commission on Testing and Public Policy (1990). *From Gatekeeper to Gateway: Transforming Testing in America*. Chestnut Hill, MA: National Commission on Testing and Public Policy, Boston College.

Noddings, N. (1984). *Caring: A Feminine Approach to Ethics and Moral Education*. Berkeley, CA: University of California Press.

Noddings, N. (1997). "A Morally Defensible Mission for the Schools in the 21st Century." In Clinchy Evans (ed.), *Transforming Public Education*. New York: Teachers College Press.

Nye, B., Hedges, L. V., and Konstantopoulos, S. (1999). "The Long-Term Effects of Small Classes: A Five-Year Follow-Up of the Tennessee Class Size Experiment." *Educational Evaluation & Policy Analysis*, 21(2), 127–142.

Oakeshott, M. (1967). "The Voice of Poetry in the Conversation of Mankind." In M. Oakeshott (ed.), *Rationalism in Politics and Other Essays*. Indianapolis: Liberty Press, pp. 483–525.

Pearson, J. (1993). *Myths of Educational Choice*. Westport, CT: Praeger.

Peters, R. S. (1966). *Ethics and Education*. London: Allen and Unwin.

Peters, R. S. (1974). *Psychology and Ethical Development*. London: Allen and Unwin.

Piaget, J. (1954). *The Construction of Reality in the Child*. New York: Basic Books.

Polanyi, M. (1962). *Personal Knowledge*. New York: Harper and Row.

Postman, N. (1984). *The Disappearance of Childhood*. New York: Dell.

Public Agenda Foundation (1998). *A Lot to Be Thankful For: What Parents Want Children to Learn about America*. New York: Public Agenda Foundation.

Rich, J. M. and DeVitis, J. L. (1992). *Competition in Education*. Springfield, IL: Charles C. Thomas.

Romano, L. (1999). "Oklahoma's Divisive Disclaimer on Evolution." *Washington Post*, December 1, p. A03.

Rugg, H. (ed.) (1926). *Curriculum Making Past and Present*, The 27th Yearbook of the National Society of Education. Chicago: National Society for the Study of Education.

Sandia National Laboratories (1993). "Perspectives on Education in America: An Annotated Briefing." *Journal of Educational Research*, 86, 59–310.

Sarason, S. B. (1998). *Charter Schools: Another Flawed Educational Reform?* New York: Teachers College Press.

Schon, D. A. and Rein, M. (1994). *Frame Reflection: Towards the Resolution of Intractable Policy Controversies*. New York: Basic Books.

Schulte, B. (1999). "Divided on Connected Math: For Some Parents and Experts, Curriculum Doesn't Add Up." *Washington Post*, October 17.

Sears, J. T. (1998). "Crossing Boundaries and Becoming the Other: Voices Across Borders." In J. T. Sears and J. C. Carper (eds), *Curriculum, Religion, and Public Education*. New York: Teachers College Press.

Shaklee, B. D., Barbour, N. E., Ambrose, R., and Hansford, S. J. (1997). *Designing and Using Portfolios*. Needham Heights, MA: Allyn and Bacon.

Slavin, R. E. (1990). *Cooperative Learning: Theory, Research, and Practice*. Englewood Cliffs, NJ: Prentice Hall.

Sockett, H. (1993). *The Moral Base for Teacher Professionalism*. New York: Teachers College Press.

Sockett, H., DeMulder, E., LePage, P., and Wood, D. (2001). *Transforming Teacher Education: Lessons in Professional Development*. Westport, CT: Bergin and Garvey.

Sosniak, L. A. and Ethington, C. A. (1992). "When Public School Choice Is Not Academic: Findings from the National Educational Longitudinal Study of 1988." *Educational Evaluation and Policy Analysis*, 14, 33–52.

Stearns, P. N. (1993). *Meaning Over Memory: Recasting the Teaching of Culture and History*. Chapel Hill, NC: University of North Carolina Press.

Strike, K. A. (1999). "Justice, Caring and Universality: In Defense of Moral Pluralism." In S. Katz, N. Noddings, and K. A. Strike (eds), *Justice and Caring: The Search for Common Ground in Education*. New York: Teachers College Press.

Tannen, D. (1993). *You Just Don't Understand*. New York: Ballantine Books.

Tannen, D. (1998). *The Argument Culture: Stopping America's War of Words*. New York: Ballantine Books.

Vygotsky, L. S. (1986). *Thought and Language*. Cambridge, MA: MIT Press.

Washington Times (1994). "Reporting on the Release by the College Board of 1994 SAT Scores." *Washington Times*, August 25, p. A4.

Yancey, P. (2000). *Parents Founding Charter Schools. Dilemmas of Empowerment and Decentralization*. New York: Peter Lang.

Young, T. W. and Clinchy, E. (1992). *Choice in Public Education*. New York: Teachers College Press.

Zoborfsky, L. and Hauser, J. (1996). "Choice in Assessment." Unpublished research report, Institute for Educational Transformation Project, George Mason University.

Index